The
Great Western Railway
in
East Cornwall

Alan Bennett

Published by
Runpast Publishing
8 Gwernant Road, Cheltenham, Gloucestershire GL51 5ES

To my wife Josephine

Designed by Roger Hardingham
© Alan Bennett & Runpast Publishing   ISBN 1 870754 11 5   1990
Typeset by PageMerger, Southampton
Printed by Amadeus Press, Huddersfield, West Yorkshire

Introduction

Railway development in East Cornwall during the early 1840s was characterised by the disputes and rivalries of two greatly conflicting interests. The area became something of a battle ground, vital territory to be fought for, as both the broad gauge Cornwall Railway and the standard gauge Devon and Cornwall Central Railway sought to extend their lines westward through the county. Historical and geographical considerations had determined that, in East Cornwall, the demands of the landscape and of future economic viability would be decisive in the development of railway initiatives.

In the event, the Cornwall Railway with its southerly route, built to the broad gauge, emerged victorious. The main line through the county was, therefore, to run westward from Plymouth to the satisfaction of the many communities soon to benefit from its presence. This debate as to the appropriate route for the railway to the west is of itself sufficient to justify interest in the area. It was certainly one of the definitive issues when considering the railway history.

East Cornwall as defined here covers the largely rural landscape reaching from the Tamar at Saltash, westward to Lostwithiel. With the exception of the Caradon district during its time as a leading copper producer, East Cornwall was somewhat sparsely populated with many widespread communities looking to agriculture as the main way of life. Looe was the main fishing port and shipping centre in the coastal district eastward to the Tamar and, with the active assistance of the GWR this century, the town developed as a tourist resort.

As mentioned above, it was as a through route on the main line that the area gained its greatest significance. A very useful extra for this was the fact also that the line passed through some extremely beautiful countryside, rich and varied in type; a factor that had certainly not been lost on the early promoters, nor on the GWR publicists anxious for a positive image.

Launceston, an obviously important Cornish community at the border, has not been included in this survey. Its story, as understood in the context of GWR development belongs, eventually, to a volume on West Devon. In social and economic terms the early railway initiative at Launceston linked the line with the communities of West Devon, reaching down, via Tavistock, to Plymouth. Train services over this route to Launceston began during the summer of 1865. It was the London and South Western Railway who, sometime later, gave Launceston direct connection with other Cornish towns inland and along the north coast.

Contents

Acknowledgements

Many people have helped in the preparation of this book and I would like the opportunity to thank them.

Firstly, I must mention publishers Roger Hardingham and, ultimately, Stephen Mourton, for bringing the material to print. Terry Knight and Joanne Hillman of the Cornwall Local Studies Library, Redruth, deserve special mention for all their interest and help. Peter Gray, Michael Mensing and Peter Treloar have again provided really excellent photographs for this final volume on Cornwall, and I must mention and thank Margaret Barron for typing the manuscript, together with several late additions/alterations. Thanks also to Ian Lloyd for the excellent plans.

Finally, I would like to thank my wife, Jo, for her part in encouraging me and taking an active interest in the project generally. With this in mind, I would like to dedicate the book to her.

Map of the GWR in East Cornwall

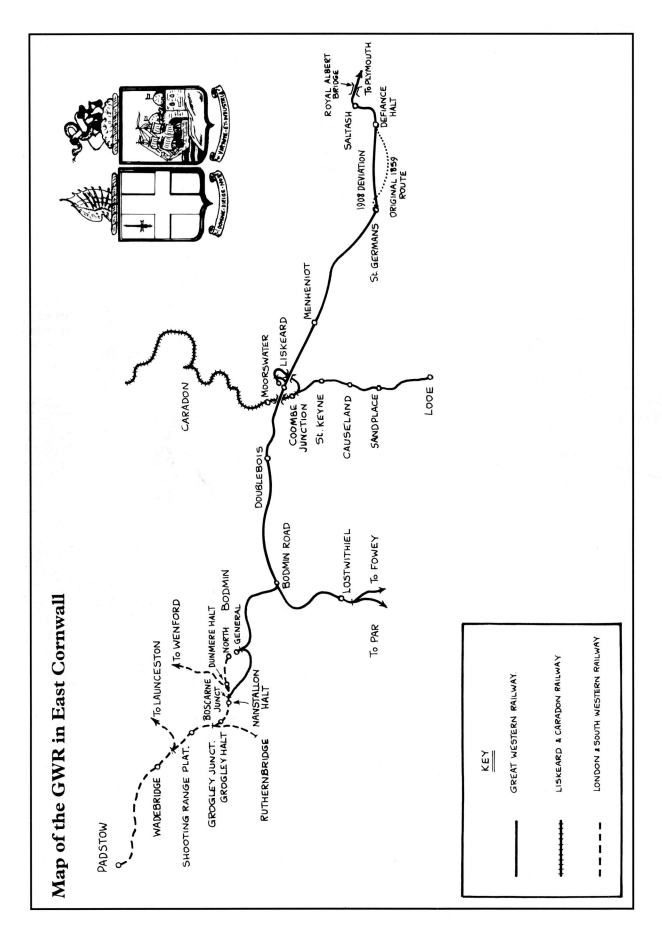

KEY

——————— GREAT WESTERN RAILWAY.

+++++++++ LISKEARD & CARADON RAILWAY.

--------- LONDON & SOUTH WESTERN RAILWAY

Chapter One

The GWR In East Cornwall

Plans for two rival railway schemes in Cornwall came before Parliament in 1845. The intention in both cases was to serve the packet port of Falmouth on the south coast and provide direct links with centres of population and industry in other parts of Britain. Whilst they shared this common aim, however, the two concerns planned to reach Falmouth over very different routes.

Both concerns required heavy engineering works. The Cornwall Railway surveyed by Captain Moorsom included provision for a ferry across the Tamar at Torpoint. Gradients and curvature were severe with sections as steep as 1 in 45. For its part, the 'Central' scheme (in many respects a re-statement of an earlier plan dating from 1836) involved massive cuttings and no less than 24 tunnels

Waiting for the train at Sandplace as photographed during the 1920s. The photograph shows a train arriving from Looe. Sandplace opened in December 1881. Note the somewhat primitive accommodation provided here – the single hut and an oil lamp. The locomotive here is GWR 4-4-0 ST No. 13 loaned to the line in 1909 and working for various periods thereafter.   *Cornwall Local Studies Library*

The rivals were the Cornwall Railway, offering a southerly coastal route from Plymouth, and the Devon and Cornwall Central Railway, which was intent upon a line westward from Exeter, entering the county at Launceston and following the central upland districts to Bodmin and thence to Truro and Falmouth. The Cornwall Railway was a broad gauge concern backed by the Great Western and Bristol and Exeter companies, and was to link directly with the South Devon Railway (opened 2nd April 1849) at Plymouth. By contrast, the Devon and Cornwall Central was to be a standard gauge line, supported at a distance by the London and South Western Railway.

through granite formations as it negotiated the formidable terrain of Bodmin Moor on its way westward to Truro. Opponents offered allusions to classical history: 'Since the days of Xerxes who attempted to tunnel Mount Athos to take his fleet through, so wild a scheme was never dreamt of!'

In the event, Parliament favoured the Cornwall Railway and its coastal route. The Board of Trade could not sanction the massive engineering works needed by the rival project and they further criticised the Central scheme on commercial grounds, given that the major towns and bulk of the population was towards the south coast. Having passed the

Commons, however, the Cornwall project was rejected by a Committee of the House of Lords which found itself unable to allow the line to be built whilst it intended to ferry its trains across the Tamar by 'moveable bridge worked by machinery'. The severe gradients also gave cause for concern, leaving the Cornwall Railway to consider suitable alternatives.

As the newly appointed engineer to the line, replacing Captain Moorsom, Brunel prepared a new survey for submission in 1846. He made detailed changes particularly east of St Germans. Instead of the ferry idea at Torpoint, Brunel planned to bridge the Tamar further up-river at Saltash, which meant planning a revised route to St Germans. The severity of the gradients overall was brought down to 1 in 57 and 1 in 60 at worst, but Brunel emphasised that whatever the route, the main line through the county would inevitably involve heavy gradients and severe curvature.

The new plans were offered to Parliament, and this time, despite considerable opposition from many hostile interests within and beyond the county, the Cornwall Railway gained its Act. It was Incorporated on 3rd August 1846, with capital of £160,000 and subscriptions from the Great Wester, theBristol and Exeter, and the South Devon Railway of £75,000, £112,000 and £150,000 respectively. A double track, broad gauge line was to be built 'from a junction with the South Devon Railway in the Parish of St Andrew, Plymouth, to the Town of Falmouth in the Parish of Budock.' Branches were also to be built from the main line into Bodmin itself and to the quays at Newham (Truro) and at Penryn. Connection and a lease was planned for the Liskeard and Caradon mineral line, together with somewhat similar arrangements for the Bodmin and Wadebridge line, where it hoped to extend to Padstow on the north coast.

Amongst the many arguments put forward by the Cornwall Railway for its southerly coastal route was that stressing the image and impact of the landscape itself. The Cornwall Company deliberately emphasised the 'rich, varied and romantic character' of its line as against what it termed the 'wastes, deserts and marshes' defining the Central route. The character and appeal of the 'coastal' line, according to its supporters, came not only from social and economic consideration but also through aesthetic appreciation. Whilst the dreary and desolate landscape of the Central route, it was argued, could do little to promote the best interests of the county, it could well present a false and damaging impression to the traveller.

With direct reference to the existing coach road through the county, crossing Goss Moor and Bodmin Moor, and following a similar route to that for the proposed Central line, *The Royal Cornwall Gazette* of May 1859 made the following observation:

> The course of the road as little represents the character of the County as Dartmoor does of Devon, but the wearied and disgusted traveller did not know this; and it was by this road that all the passengers by packet ship travelled to and from Falmouth. No wonder that Cornwall was stigmatised as a West Barbary when such a 'Sahara' was the specimen presented.

By contrast, the newspaper spoke most favourably of the newly opened Cornwall Railway:

> The present line of Railway will lead to a very different estimate. All scenery, the richest in fertility, the fairest in woodland, the most interesting for unceasing variety and romatic character, the most animated as a picture of science, and industry, and, last, not least, for moral charm is after all the greatest of the landscape, the appearance of order and intelligence in the numerous population and delight the traveller all along the line.

Civilisation and progress were associates of the new railway in an obvious harmony of interest. *The Royal Cornwall Gazette* was, of course, no disinterested commentator as far as the Cornwall Railway was concerned, but these extracts do offer interesting contemporary insights into the impact of the railway within the community and its inter-relationship with the landscape.

A panoramic view showing Brunel's famous structure across the Tamar and the lesser known Coombe-by-St Stephen Viaduct, immediately south of Saltash station. The photograph shows the consideravle curvature through the station, bringing down trains, as seen here, from a westward to a southerly direction parallel with the river. 4-6-0s Nos. 1021 *County of Montgomery* and 7816 *Frilsham Manor*, head the 10.35 am Paddington – Penzance. Note the length of this train, the rear coaches having just passed the platforms. This 10.35 Paddington departure made up one part of the 'Cornish Riviera Express' on Summer Saturdays. *P. Gray*

Chapter Two

Construction and Opening

Having celebrated the passing of the Act the Cornwall Railway was almost immediately faced with an acute financial crisis, part of a widespread national depression in trade and industry. Many railway projects originating from the recent 'Railway Mania' fell victim to the crisis, not least the Cornwall Railway which was anything but prosperous. Faced with demands they could not meet, large numbers of shareholders defaulted on their commitments, with the local press carrying detailed coverage of the forfeiture on Company shares.

Very little in the way of construction had been achieved by 1850, but by 1852 steps were taken to ease the financial problems. It was decided to build a single, broad gauge line and shareholders were told in April 1852 that plans and proposals for the various branches and extensions, mentioned above, were to be abandoned with the sanction of the Board of Trade. Capital was also to be reduced from £1,600,000 to £1,250,000 with £50 shares cut to £20. Three years later, in June 1855, with the line far from complete, the Company entered into a saving agreement with the Associated Companies – the Great Western, Bristol and Exeter, and South Devon Railways – whereby they leased the line, easing the financial burdens.

Progress was made with the placing of the contract for works between Truro and St Austell in the summer of 1852, and by the beginning of the new year this contract, with Messrs Sharpe and Son, was extended to cover the section from St Austell to Liskeard. East of the Tamar, the contract was also let for the line between Devonport and the river itself, the work being carried out by H & H Drew. Good progress was reported on this latter section by July 1853 when it was said that much of the levelling and cutting had taken place.

The most exacting task, however, was that of bridging the Tamar itself, the directors being pleased to place the contract for this work in January 1853. Brunel had chosen to cross the river at Saltash and at this location the Tamar is 1,100 feet wide and 80 feet deep at its maximum. To link Devon and Cornwall across this great natural county boundary demanded engineering abilities of the highest order.

Charles J Mare, well known for his work on Stephenson's Britannia Bridge across the Menai Straits, and for the construction of iron ships at Blackwall, was awarded the contract for the bridge. He agreed to build it for £162,000 and to complete the work in two years and four months. His initial task, however, was to establish all the necessary workshops and yards along the Devon shore. *The West Briton* of September 1853 described the scene at riverside:

The preparatory works for this stupendous undertaking, the contract for the erection of which has been taken by Mr C.J. Mare, of Blackwall, are being prosecuted with great vigour. Already the once quiet spot known as Saltash Passage is converted into a place of bustle and business. Extensive workshops and smithies have been erected. Steam machinery of every description for planing, rolling into shape, cutting, drilling, and punching the masses of iron to form parts of the bridge, is in full operation. The smiths' shop contains eight

forges, worked upon the principle of exhaustion, of what is commonly called fan bellows, driven by steam. A long slip, similar to that used for ship building has been laid down, for the construction of the cylinders intended to be sunk in the river, for raising the centre pieces of the bridge. The one now being built is to be thirty seven feet in diameter and eighty five feet deep; when completed it will be launched and sunk into position, and being closed at about thirty feet from the top, will, in fact, be a huge diving bell, and the men working within it supplied with air on the same principle as that adopted with the ordinary bell.

Whilst the work proceeded on the Devon shore, the contract for construction of the masonry piers, ten on the Cornish side and, eventually, seven on the Devon side, went ahead. The granite was supplied by Mr Meredith, representative of the late J.T. Treffry of Fowey and the work was carried out by Mr Willcocks who had previously built the viaduct at Ivybridge on the South Devon Railway. The foundation for the first pier at Saltash was laid on 4th July 1853 with something of a ceremony.

When work on the great cylinder for the central pier had been completed it was towed out to its position and sunk, with great accuracy, in June 1854. Brunel gave details of the work in his Engineer's Report to the Company for August of that year:

The Iron Cylinder, intended to serve as a Cofferdam for the Centre Pier, – containing within itself all the arrangements of air chambers, passages etc, necessary for using it either as a large diving bell, or simply as a Cofferdam, as circumstances might require, and so constructed as to be afterwards divided into two parts vertically, and removed after the pier shall have been built within it, the whole weighing upwards of 300 tons, was safely launched and floated into place where it was raised perpendicularly, and pitched upon its lower edge into the centre of the river. The river is at this point upwards of 50 feet deep at low water, of neap tides, and except for a short time on the turn of the tide there is a considerable current. Under such circumstances, this cylinder, drawing 50 feet of water, was pitched with its lower edge accurately, that is, within three or four inches of the exact point required. –

Since then, the work has been carried on at the bottom of the cylinder as in a diving bell, against a pressure of water occasionally of 70 feet and 80 feet. The mud and other deposits forming the bed of the river for 10 or 12 feet in thickness have been removed and the cylinder is now excavating the rock into level beds for receiving the masonry. In superintending this work, involving as it does, great bodily exertion and exposure to cold and wet under pressure of air that many cannot endure, and a work not entirely free from risk, I am indebted to the able and constant assistances of Mr Brereton, who has taken up residence at Plymouth for a time for that purpose –

During the following summer, the Company determined upon completing the line between Plymouth and

The Royal Albert Bridge floodlit for its centenary in the summer of 1959.

P. Gray

Truro, making this their priority. The contract was also let for the section between Liskeard and Saltash in August 1855. More problems ensued at the bridge, however, when in October 1855 the contractor, C.J. Mare, failed, bringing work to a temporary halt.

Elsewhere news was mixed. By early 1856 it was reported that, between Truro and Liskeard, only Largin and St Pinnock viaducts needed further timberworks, but there were also reports of faults with Moorswater viaduct immediately west of Liskeard. The piers had failed to meet requirements and needed to be rebuilt. This was completed by the autumn of 1856. Good news from Brunel's report to the Company in August 1856 came with the statement that, at the Tamar, the work on the central pier was now within a few feet of the high water mark. The autumn of 1856 also saw this most difficult of works completed. Further encouragement came with the completion of work between Truro and Liskeard; this section now being ready for the permanent way.

In the Report to the Company in February 1857 Brunel emphasised the all-important effort needed at the bridge:

'It is to the Bridge that all our exertions have been and must be applied.'

Some six months later, on Tuesday 1st September, the first of the two great tubes or spans, that for the Cornwall side, was floated into position. Having been constructed in the yards on the Devon shore it had to be positioned on piers in the river prior to the long business of lifting it, by hydraulic presses, to its correct height giving a clearance of 100 feet above the high water mark.

The Royal Cornwall Gazette covered the events of 1st September in some detail. A useful description of the work and procedure was included:

This Bridge is to be altogether 2,000 feet in length, the span of each main opening being from the centre of one pier to the centre of the other, 455 feet. – The main openings are each spanned by an oval tube whose diameters are 16 feet 9 inches by 12 feet 3 inches, the ends of which are connected by chains which form a parabolic curve, and from those chains are suspended the roadway. To prevent the sacking down of the tube, at intervals of 40 feet occur vertical strutts for the purpose of distributing the load. – These sections when fixed in their permanent positions will stand with their shore ends on brick pillars, surmounting granite and limestone piers, and their other ends on standards supported by four hollow octangonal cast iron columns, ten feet in diameter, and resting on a solid granite circular pillar 35 feet in diameter built in the centre of the river and standing 12 feet above the high water mark – two of the columns supporting each section. From the bottom of the roadway to the top of the tube at the centre is about 75 feet, and the whole is constructed of malleable iron plates.

The section of the bridge has been constructed on a temporary quay by the water's edge, and docks were cut under a stage erected for the admission of two pontoons at each end. These pontoons draw about eight feet six inches of water, one foot of immersion beyond their natural draft being equal to 250 tons or thereabouts. By means of valves the pontoons admit water into their interiors and were thus passed beneath the ends of the tube; and on closing those valves they rose with the tide and raised their ponderous weight. At the ends of the tubes bed plates and rollers allow of their free extension and contraction under varying temperatures. –

It was obviously a great day for the local population in particular. From estimates it was claimed that nearly 10,000 people were brought to Saltash by steamers from Devonport. The South Devon Railway also brought large numbers of people to witness the events and by the afternoon, of this 'grand and general holiday occasion' at least 20,000 were said to be in attendance. The Company's yards on both sides of the river were enclosed for special viewing purposes, admission being available by ticket. This was organised by the Company Secretary, Mr Bond. A large number of yachts and steamers were on the river, giving their passengers an excellent view, whilst on the Devon shore, long rows of refreshment stalls and some show-tents were erected. 'A bountiful luncheon' was provided in the Stores area on the Saltash side for the many distinguished guests who included the management of the Cornwall, South Devon and Bristol and Exeter Railways, leading civic figures; a large body of the neighbouring gentry, and representatives from the Admiralty.

The business of floating the great tube into position took a little over two hours, but was the end result of considerable planning. Details were given by the press:

During the past week extensive preparations were made, under the superintendence of Mr Brunel and his engineering staff; – Five vessels, borrowed from the Government authorities, were moored in a semi circle above the bridge, on board of which were powerful crabs for the purpose of warping the tube round to its position. A large portion of the gear employed and appliances used was borrowed from the Dockyard; but Mr Canning of Teat's Hill supplied the rope used in controlling the pontoons. Captain Claxton, RN, who had charge of the floating of the Menai and Conway bridges was present to supervise everything afloat, Mr Brunel taking the entire control of the pontoons and directing operations by means of signals and flags. –

Each of the vessels used for the work carried its particular number for easy identification and reference. Brunel directed operations from a specially built platform at the centre of the truss. The main business of the day was completed in a little over two hours and was timed to coincide with the high tide. Having been hauled out across the river and turned through a quarter of a circle the truss was positioned securely between the western and central piers. The valves were then opened admitting water into the

pontoons and allowing them to sink, and with the tide falling at just after 3.30 pm the tube rested on its piers. At 5 pm the Royal Marines Band, stationed on a steamer alongside the tube, played the National Anthem, marking the end of the proceedings. The crowds dispersed gradually, aware of the fact that they had witnessed a significant achievement, not only in engineering terms, but in long term social and economic development also.

Early in the following year Brunel reported that the span had been lifted and the piers built up at the rate of six feet a week. He also informed the Company that the floor or roadway of the bridge was now about 54 feet above the ordinary spring tides. Further good news came via this February report. With reference to the works elsewhere on the line he wrote:

Upon the whole of the rest of the line, little beyond the superstructure of the Liskeard viaduct and the timber viaducts between and St Germans, and the piling and superstructures of St Germans viaduct remains to be completed.

The laying of the permanent way is about to be commenced.

As a central point on the Cornwall Railway, Lostwithiel was chosen as the depot for the incoming timber and rails. The sleepers were to be cut to the required size at the depot and distributed along the line with the minimum of delay.

The second great tube for the Tamar Bridge was floated successfully on 10th July 1858. Brunel did not supervise the work on this occasion due to illness, the operations being controlled by his gifted assistant, R.P. Brereton. Again, the work was conducted in silence with all necessary instructions being made by flag signals and careful numbering of all equipment for easy identification. Five vessels and a number of blue jackets from Her Majesty's ship *Exmouth* were also involved. As previously, Captain Claxton took charge of the ships and their operations. According to reports, the second great tube was safely lodged on the river piers by 5 pm. The work of raising it began soon after, this being completed by March 1859.

In the half-yearly report of February 1859 the Company Secretary, Mr Bond, was able at last to make the following statement:

The Royal Albert Bridge is now an accomplished fact – a beautiful and substantial structure which affords a wonderful proof of the most successful application of mechanical science to overcome the greatest natural difficulty connected with the construction of your Railway.

Brunel also reported that the works between Plymouth and Saltash had been completed within the last half year and that, further westward, a locomotive had been brought onto the railway at Par and was working ballast trains of up to 160 tons between Truro and Liskeard. Ballast workings proved useful in consolidating the embankments and testing the viaducts. The Royal Albert Bridge was also tested by running heavy trains across it.

The first train from Plymouth to Truro ran on 11 April 1859 shortly before the official inspection by the Board of Trade.

Having given permission in August 1853 for it to be named after him, H.R.H. Prince Albert officially opened the

Bridge on 2nd May 1859. This was obviously another great occasion attracting, yet again, many thousands of spectators and giving rise to considerable festivities and ceremonial. Brunel was not present, by this time his health had deteriorated considerably and he had wintered in the warm Mediterranean climate. On his return to England he did make a personal inspection of the bridge. Because of his medical condition he was confined to a couch which had been specially fitted to an open wagon. This vehicle was propelled across the bridge enabling Brunel to make his inspection and to savour his achievement – his last great railway work. He died, not long afterwards, on 5th September 1859. The inscription: 'I K BRUNEL, ENGINEER, 1859', was placed over both the western and eastern archways of the Royal Albert Bridge before the end of that year. Put there by the Directors of the Cornwall Railway it was a further tribute to the brilliant engineer whose work had been so closely associated with railway development in the West Country.

Together with regular routine maintenance the Royal Albert Bridge has received some detailed attention this century. Cross girders were incorporated to cope with the increasing weight of trains, and in 1908 the two wrought iron spans at the western end of the bridge were replaced improving the approach in conjunction with developments at Saltash station. All the other fifteen wrought iron spans were also replaced twenty years later. Beginning in March 1927, mild steel spans were substituted for the original wrought iron structures with the work commencing on the Devon side. In the post-war period there were further developments, including, in 1968, strengthening of the two main trusses. Additional horizontal bracing was provided whilst the vertical ties were also strengthened by the use of much heavier sectioned steel.

A view of the Royal Albert Bridge as seen in an 1859 print, looking towards the riverside community of Saltash. The print was clearly intended to celebrate the great engineering achievement in spanning the River Tamar but it also emphasises the scene in which the bridge was located. Whilst men are shown working in the foreground, on the Devon side, a train crosses the bridge from Saltash high above the houses nearest the river. The cattle also serve to express a strong sense of the rural landscape. As such, these contemporary prints can often offer us an excellent insight into the prevailing altitudes and atmosphere of the time showing the relationship between the railway, the community and the landscape.
Penzance Library

Chapter Three

The Main Line: Saltash – Lostwithiel

Saltash station and the Royal Albert Bridge together make an excellent gateway to and from Cornwall. The station is immediately beyond the western end of the Royal Albert itself with the platforms running right to the bridge. A tight curve takes the line off the bridge and through the station bringing trains round from a westerly direction in crossing the Tamar to a southerly route along the hillside above the river.

The main buildings at Saltash, dating from development in the 1880s, were on the 'up' side with a goods yard and shed, again on the 'up' side, at the west end of the station. A signalbox was also sited approximately mid way along the 'up' platform, the latter being extended in 1908. Beyond the station the line crosses Coombe by Saltash viaduct. The original structure here was of timber carrying a single line and was 201 yards in length and 86 feet high. A masonry construction replaced the timber viaduct in 1894. In February 1906 the section from Saltash to Wearde Siding signal box was doubled. This section of line has been considered elsewhere in the coverage of the 1908 deviation, Saltash – St Germans, but it is worth mention here that the distance from Saltash was 73 chains and that the box was sited on the south side of the line, opposite the siding. Apparatus for lineside distribution of mail was also installed opposite the siding at the turn of the century.

From Wearde siding the original Cornwall Railway route ran south-westward close to the River Lynher. The first of several creeks was bridged at Antony Passage. Forder viaduct, built of timber, was 202 yards in length and 67 feet high. For a considerable distance west of Forder the line ran on an embankment, initially, very close to the river bank. Wivelscombe viaduct also crossed a creek, with considerable expanses of salt marsh to the south. The viaduct was 66 yards long and 25 feet high. To the south, across the salt marsh, Ince Castle stood guard over the waters.

Almost one mile west of Wivelscombe, approximately mid-way between the latter and Grove viaduct, was Wivelscombe signal box. From this point the line turned to the north-west on a somewhat arduous climb ascending to and beyond St Germans at gradients varying between 1 in 62 and 1 in 76. Grove viaduct, the smallest on this section of line, followed. It was 38 yards long and 29 feet high.

'4300' class 2-6-0 No. 6301 crosses the Royal Albert to enter Saltash station on 2nd May 1959, exactly 100 years after the official opening of the bridge by Prince Albert. The train is the 5.30 am Paddington – Penzance, the photograph being taken from the 'down' platform.

P. Gray

Watched by a member of the staff and possibly a young admirer, 4-6-0 No. 6849 *Walton Grange* comes off the Royal Albert Bridge into Saltash station with the 3.40 pm Plymouth – Penzance stopping train, 29th September 1959. The two nearest spans of the bridge, shown here, were rebuilt in 1908, widening the approach. All the remaining spans were replaced in 1927.
P. Gray

A full view looking towards Plymouth with '6400' class 0-6-0 pannier tank No. 6420 crossing Forder viaduct. The train is the 5.50 pm auto service from Plymouth to Liskeard, on 31st July 1959. Forder viaduct is well illustrated here, as is a section of the original Cornwall Railway route from Saltash to St Germans. This is marked by the bridge to the right of centre and the track alignment running through the field to the right. Note also the aircraft-carrier and various other warships at anchor.
P. Gray

Double-heading in exquisite countryside, 4-6-0 No. 6931, *Aldborough Hall* and No. 6826 *Nannerth Grange*, have just crossed Forder viaduct with the 10.00 am Newquay – Paddington on 25th July 1959. Trematon Castle can be seen on the hill on the right of the photograph, looking down on the viaduct and the line.   *P. Gray*

Notter viaduct was approached on an embankment, again, with evidence of salt marsh nearby. The viaduct carried the line over the River Lynher, the latter running north-south at this location. Notter was a substantial structure, being 307 yards long and 67 feet high. St Germans viaduct, further west, crossed the River Tiddy; it was the largest of the tidal structures at 315 yards in length and 106 feet high. Given the difficulties with mud in the creeks, all the tidal viaducts required deep foundations reaching down to 70 feet in certain cases. With the exception of Grove viaduct, these tidal structures also differed from the other early viaducts through Cornwall in that they were built entirely from timber.

Like Menheniot, to the west, St Germans station was built on a reverse curve. The main buildings were on the 'up' side with a goods yard and shed to the east of the station also on the 'up' side. St Germans signal box was at the east end of the station on the 'down' side. Between St Germans and Liskeard the main line runs north-westward climbing for almost the entire distance at gradients as steep as 1 in 78, 1 in 74 and 1 in 68, for example. Over this distance of some 8½ miles only the last 1½ are on a falling gradient although west-bound trains had some relief from the mile of level ground immediately east of Menheniot.

Two viaducts were required on the level section leading to Menheniot. The first of these was Tresulgan, 175 yards long and 93 feet in height. This timber structure was replaced by a masonry viaduct in March 1899. Coldrennick viaduct, almost immediately east of Menheniot station carried the line over the River Seaton. The original structure here was 265 yards long and 138 feet high. It was rebuilt in 1897, the timbers being replaced by brickwork built onto the original masonry piers. Iron decking rested on this brickwork, but in 1933 the iron was itself replaced by steel decking. (See also chapter on Accidents.) Between St Germans and Menheniot the line was doubled in two stages. The section from St Germans to the approach to Tresulgan viaduct was doubled in December 1895, and that from the west end of the viaduct to Menheniot, in January 1898. The line was doubled across Tresulgan viaduct in October 1898.

The St Germans – Menheniot section at 5 miles 37 chains was the longest on the entire Paddington – Penzance route for much of the inter-war period until a new signal box was provided at Trerule in 1938, dividing the section. Trerule box eventually closed in 1954.

Menheniot station, sited on a reverse curve, served the community of that name which lay just over a mile to the north of the line. The main buildings were on the 'down'

A delightful view of the Forder viaduct and its magnificent rural setting. This is a superb photograph of the railway in the glorious East Cornwall landscape. The river, fields, trees, cattle and the church tower at St Stephen all combine to make this an outstanding illustration. The train is a westbound goods headed, rather unusually for Cornwall, by '2884' class 2-8-0 No. 3862. *P. Gray*

Deep cuttings were a particular feature of the 1908 deviation line between Saltash and St Germans. Here 4-6-0 No. 1023 *County of Oxford* enters one such cutting having just crossed Forder viaduct, seen in the distance. The train, as one would expect from the stock, is the 12.05 pm Plymouth – Truro stopping service. *P. Gray*

No. 6988 Swithland Hall seen just east of Notter viaduct on the straight section leading away from Shillingham tunnel. This was to be one of the longest stretches of straight track in the county when opened in 1908. Shillingham tunnel, just visible through the smoke, was 452 yards long and was completed in 1907. 7th August 1961.
P. Gray

side being designed after the style of the South Devon Railway. A signal box was also provided on the 'down' platform, with a small yard running in behind it, entered from the west. Developments in the 1930s at Menheniot came with the provision of sidings to serve Clicker Tor Quarry, immediately west of the station on the down side. A 'down' goods loop was also provided west of the station, beyond the quarry workings. Clicker Tor became a useful source of ballast for railway works locally and for road stone supplies. Adequate provision for sidings to handle this traffic was called for in 1928 when increasingly heavier demand was apparent.

With final reference to Menheniot, it is worth recording that for several years after the Liskeard and Looe Railway had opened its link from Liskeard station to Coombe Junction (1901) the GWR continued to advertise Menheniot as the station for Looe. A connecting omnibus service ran between this station and Looe, being advertised in the summer of 1906 as follows: Menheniot – Looe depart 1005 am, 2.20 and 5.45 pm, also 8.00 am Mondays only. Looe – Menheniot 7.54 am, 11.20 am, and 4.20 pm, also 7.20 am Mondays only. The drive to Looe, described as extremely picturesque, took some ¾ hour. Passengers with heavy luggage were advised to make the entire journey by train, via Liskeard.

Continuing westward from Menheniot, four viaducts were needed to carry the line into Liskeard. The first of these was Treviddo, 162 yards long and 101 feet high. It was rebuilt in granite for September 1898 with the main line being doubled between Menheniot and the viaduct in May 1896. One mile beyond Treviddo viaduct the line ended its stiff climb, mainly at 1 in 74, and began the descent towards Liskeard. Caruther viaduct was then crossed. This was 137 yards long and 89 feet in height. It was rebuilt for 1882. Bolitho viaduct followed, being within sight of Liskeard. The viaduct here was 182 yards long and 113 feet high and was also rebuilt in 1882. Liskeard viaduct, carrying the line across the Liskeard Valley, (and the Looe branch, from May 1901) was 240 yards in length and 150 feet high. It was rebuilt in 1894 when brickwork replaced the original timbers, with iron girders supporting the track bed. The iron work was replaced by steel in 1926.

A very short rise lifted the line into Liskeard station. To complete the story of this section it remains to say that from Treviddo viaduct to Liskeard, 2¼ miles, doubling took place for August 1896.

Liskeard station was built immediately west of the viaduct and lay to the south of the town, the road from

In this view of Notter viaduct, which crosses the tidal waters of the River Lynher, 4-6-0 No. 1004 *County of Cornwall*, has just passed No. 6988 *Swithland Hall* one of the later 1944 modified 'Halls'. The 'County' is heading the 10.45 am Penzance – Plymouth, whilst the modified 'Hall' has charge of the 1.00 pm Plymouth – Penzance. 7th August 1961. *P. Gray*

Looking west at Treslugan viaduct, the 12.05 pm auto-train from Menheniot to Plymouth is seen having crossed the viaduct on 11th July 1959. The locomotive is '6400' class 0-6-0 Pannier tank No. 6419. Note the excellent condition of the permanent way and two contrasting types of rail. Note also the delightfully rural surroundings here, as elsewhere, in East Cornwall. *P. Gray*

Tresulgan viaduct was the only other viaduct, apart from Coldrennick, on the section between St Germans and Menheniot. Here '4300' class 2-6-0 No. 6397, brings the ten coaches of the 6.50 am Paddington to Penzance across the viaduct. Motive power must have been in great demand that day (11th July 1959) or there was a locomotive failure, for it was unusual for this class of engine to work such trains alone. *P. Gray*

'6400' class 0-6-0T No. 6414 enters St Germans station with the 6.44 pm Plymouth – St Germans service, 16th July, 1956. The goods shed and yard are well illustrated here and stand on the original alignment of the 1859 route between St Germans and Saltash. St Germans goods yard handled large quantities of agricultural produce in GWR days, as the station served a widespread rural area. *R.C. Riley*

Menheniot station in the 1920s. The main buildings were on the 'down' side as seen in this view looking towards Liskeard. Note the reverse curve through the station and beyond, past the site of what became Clicker Tor Quarry, a source of plentiful ballast locally. Immediately east of the station, also on a curve, was Coldrennick viaduct rebuilt in 1897. Twelve men were killed when part of the workings collapsed during this rebuilding.
Cornwall Local Studies Library

Headed by No. 6801 *Aylburton Grange* the 12.20 pm Penzance – Kensington milk train is seen here passing Menheniot station on a bright summers day in July 1956. This locomotive was shedded at Penzance, 83G, for some time during the latter years of its working life, prior to the closure to steam in September 1962. It was one of a number of 'Granges' allocated to the depot for mixed traffic duties. Two milk trains worked eastward at that time, the 12.20 Penzance departure seen here and the later 6.20 pm service, also for Kensington. Lostwithiel was the main milk depot within the county with GWR lorry services covering all parts of Cornwall after 1932 when the Nestle's milk factory opened there.
R.C. Riley

Modified 'Hall' class No. 7916 *Mobberley Hall* takes the 1.20 pm Penzance – Paddington service through the reverse curves at Menheniot on 16th July 1956. The station buildings, signalbox and Clicker Tor Quarry are all shown here on the 'down' side. Close cooperation between the railway and the quarry was essential at Menheniot because of the proximity of the works and the line. The signalman had a special warning bell in the signalbox to ensure that he was informed of blasting times, underlining the absolute requirement to reconcile dangerous activities at the quarry with safety on the line.   *R.C. Riley*

4-6-0 No. 6873 *Caradoc Grange* takes the six coaches of an early morning stopping service to Plymouth across Liskeard viaduct on 15th August 1959. The viaduct, rebuilt in 1894, was 240 yards in length and 150 feet high. As the photograph shows, the piers were extended with brickwork, replacing the original timbers, with iron girders and, later, steel for the trackbed. The 1901 link line from Liskeard down to Coombe Junction is just hidden from view in a cutting at the bottom right corner of the illustration. Liskeard main line signalbox can be seen in the far righthand top of the picture.   *P. Gray*

Passengers awaiting an 'up' train watch as 4-6-0 No. 1023 *County of Oxford*, arrives at Liskeard with the 12.05 pm Plymouth–Truro stopper, 11th July 1959. The photograph shows that not every day was fine and sunny in the summer of 1959; nearly, but not quite. Even so, the weather adds to the atmosphere making this a definitive composition of the time. Note the realignment to the main line, (mentioned in the text) beyond the last coach. As the sign says on entry to the platform, the Looe branch was at the far end of the station to the left and at a right angle to the main line.   *P. Gray*

'4300' class 2-6-0 No. 7321 Liskeard with the 3.40 pm stopping service from Plymouth–Penzance. The main building at Liskeard was at road level, above the platform. The ticket office and other facilities can be seen as the group of buildings immediately to the left and behind the road bridge. This bridge carries the main road from Liskeard to Looe.   *M. Mensing*

Mogul '4300' class 2-6-0 No. 5350 climbs the gradient (1 in 59) past the goods shed to reach the platform at Liskeard with an 'up' freight on 14th June 1956. The goods shed appears to be enjoying business with wagons inside and various commodities stored on the platform. Today the site is waste ground.   *M. Mensing*

Liskeard to Looe passing over the main line and the platforms themselves.

The general layout at Liskeard was quite extensive even before 1901 when it became the junction for Looe. At the east end of the station there were sidings north and south of the main line. To the north, two sidings were set at right angles to the main line and were reached by means of a wagon turntable installed on the main access siding which ran eastward, parallel with the main line. The right angled alignment had certain similarities with the layout later introduced for the station and yard serving the Looe line.

South of the main line was a small single-road engine shed with coal store with a further siding immediately to the south. Access to these lines was also by means of a turntable, the latter dating from 1860. The engine shed was closed in 1918 and the site then became available for the down refuge sidings. Liskeard's signalbox was also positioned at the east end of the 'down' platform in June 1915 following the closure of the earlier box on the 'up' platform. The latter was sited between the footbridge and the road bridge carrying the Liskeard – Looe road.

With the opening of the loop to Coombe Junction it had been necessary to stagger the platform ends. The 'up' side reached further eastward because of the need on the 'down' side for clearances for traffic entering and leaving the branch. The east end of the down platform was extended in 1937 as a result of alterations to the junction with the Looe branch.

At the opposite end of the station the 'down' platform extended further westward than the 'up' side. This again was for reasons of access, in this case, entry to the goods yard and goods shed west of the station. Like the entire site, the goods yard was built in a cutting but on land that had been especially levelled for it. The main line alongside descends sharply on a gradient of 1 in 59. The wooden shed was served by two sidings with a loading platform on the north side and cattle pens set against the cutting itself. This yard was easily reached from the main road by means of a straight approach running parallel with the line.

When the route westward from Liskeard to Doublebois was doubled in February 1894 it was necessary to realign the track at the west end of the station. The new double line was a little to the south of the original single track and entailed a slight curve alongside the goods shed. This realignment gave the opportunity for a lengthy 'up' refuge siding which was provided alongside the goods shed, the new siding occupying, in part, the place of the original main line. Realignment was also evident at the opposite end of the station immediately west of Liskeard viaduct where the main line was shifted slightly southward for clearances.

Given that Liskeard station was in a cutting it was necessary to locate the main building – booking hall, station master's office, parcels office and waiting room – at road level, above the platforms. This building was on the 'up' side with the main entrance facing along Station Road in the direction of the town.

A fine view of the west end of Liskeard station taken from the foot/trolley bridge. No. 6879 *Overton Grange* passes through with a 'down' freight whilst in the goods yard '5700' class 0-6-0 pannier tank No. 3686 goes about its business with a pick-up freight. The gas lamps, water tower, barrows, semaphore signals and the people standing and watching from the platform and the road bridge give this photograph a tremendous sense of period, characterising the mid and later 1950s. Notice also the steep gradient at 1 in 59 and the sharp curve entering and leaving the station.

M. Mensing

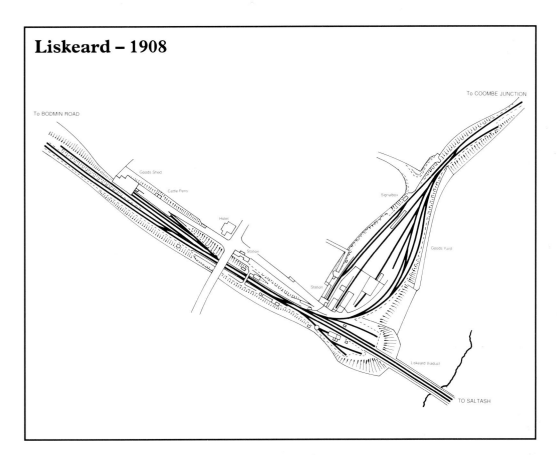

Liskeard – 1908

'4575' class 2-6-2T No. 5532 takes water at the west end of the 'down' platform having worked in on the evening Plymouth–Liskeard stopping service. The photograph offers useful detail on the goods shed and its yard.

P. Gray

The sharp curve leading away from Moorswater viaduct near Liskeard. Here 4-6-0 No. 6931 *Aldborough Hall* and '4300' class 2-6-0 No. 6301 bring the 9.30 am Paddington–Newquay off the viaduct and face a climb of 2¾ miles, largely at 1 in 70, westward to Double-bois. Moorswater viaduct, rebuilt in 1881, looks very much part of the land-scape here, which like East Cornwall generally, is lush, predominantly rural in kind. *P. Gray*

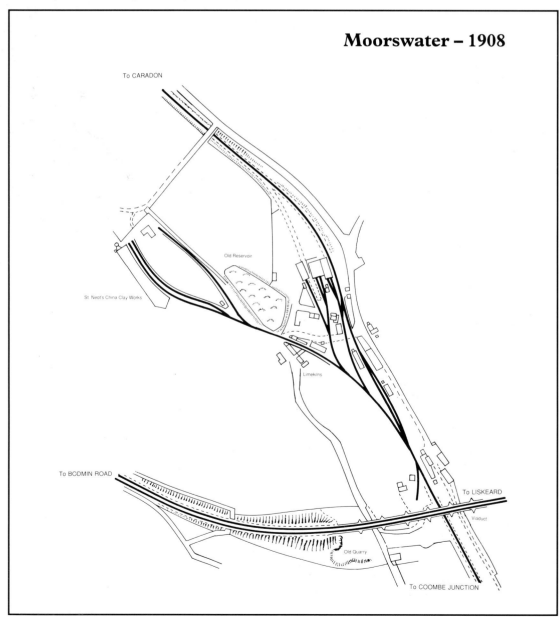

Moorswater – 1908

To CARADON

Old Reservoir

St. Neot's China Clay Works

Limekilns

To BODMIN ROAD

To LISKEARD

Viaduct

Old Quarry

To COOMBE JUNCTION

Moorswater again; this time looking northward from Coombe Junction on the Looe branch. An unidentified 'Hall' crosses the viaduct eastward with a six coach service bound for Plymouth, 2nd August 1958. The original piers for the wooden viaduct can be seen here alongside the splendid 1881 rebuild. Moorswater was 318 yards long and 147 feet high.   *P. Gray*

Leaving Liskeard the main line falls at 1 in 59 for ½ mile to Moorswater viaduct. The piers of the original structure here are to the south of the line. At 318 yards in length and 147 feet high Moorswater viaduct carried the line over the Liskeard and Looe Railway, with Caradon Company's locomotive shed and workshop to the north, and Coombe Junction, opened in 1901, to the south. Moorswater viaduct was rebuilt in 1881.

From Moorswater Viaduct the line climbs for much of the next 2¾ miles to Doublebois and the summit of the journey westward from the Tamar to almost sea level at Lostwithiel. The gradients average 1 in 70 but include sections as fierce as 1 in 58 to reach Doublebois station. Opened in 1860, this station was reasonably well sited to serve the community of Dobwalls, a short distance to the east, and the small settlement of Doublebois itself, immediately north of the line. The main building at the station was on the 'up' side, the entire site being located in a shallow cutting. West of the station on the 'down' side was the original goods yard of 1860 used for the practice of dividing trains (where necessary) ascending and descending the

formidable bank to and from Bodmin Road. Extreme care was required when shunting at Doublebois to avoid runaway wagons on the bank. To the east, also on the 'down' side, an extensive War Department layout was opened during World War Two. Sidings here ran eastward, parallel with the main line, whilst others turned away almost at right angles. These sidings also ran behind the 'down' platform making for a wide cutting in the station area itself. By the 1950s the east yard was used for permanent way sidings. An 'up' goods loop was also opened at Tremabe, just over a mile east of Doublebois, in July 1943, closing in 1952.

From Doublebois the line descends sharply through what could be called viaduct country, passing magnificent woodland areas and thick plantations of rhododendrons. The constant succession of viaducts, the River Fowey and the elevated nature of the route generally adds to the attraction here making this part of the journey to Lostwithiel one of the finest in Britain.

Alongside the goods yard west of Doublebois station a stop board warned all westbound goods and mineral workings to stop dead and pin down brakes. The gradients for

Doublebois station seen here on 4th July 1959 with 4-6-0 No. 5021 *Whittington Castle* passing through with the 'up' Royal Duchy', Penzance–Paddington. Extra coaches have been added at the front of the train given the demand for holiday travel on Saturdays at that time. In 1958 Doublebois still retained its early 'Cornwall Railway' notice board on the 'up' platform; today there is nothing of the station to be seen in this cutting.   *P. Gray*

A valuable photograph here that records not only steam working hard on a busy Summer Saturday, but also the last Cornwall Railway signalbox to remain standing. The entire location looks very different today, but Peter Gray's view of 4-6-0s Nos. 1021 *County of Montgomery* and 6808 *Beenham Grange* on the 9.20 am Saturdays St Ives to Paddington on 2nd August 1958, serves to remind us just how much has changed, on and off the tracks. The location is Westwood, approaching the summit at Doublebois.   *P. Gray*

Almost there! 4-6-0s Nos. 6858 *Woolston Grange* and 6849 *Walton Grange* (with smaller tender) are almost at the summit. Both drivers are looking up the gradient with their locomotives in full cry. The train is the 10.00 am Newquay–Paddington with a load of 15 coaches, 2nd August 1958. Nearby, on the 'down' side, was the site of Westwood quarry which supplied stone for rebuilding the viaducts.

P. Gray

4-6-0 Modified Hall No. 6988 *Swithland Hall* is seen here having just crossed Largin viaduct with the six coaches of the 7.40 am St Austell to Wolverhampton on 19th July 1958. The scenery here is typical of the six mile section between Bodmin Road and Doublebois; one of the most beautiful stretches of line in Britain. Lonely Largin box, at the far side of the viaduct, is still operative today but now controls a single line section across this viaduct and at St Pinnock to the east. The singling in 1964 was introduced as an alternative to economise on maintenance on these two viaducts.

P. Gray

The thirteen of the 11.10 am Penzance–Wolverhampton are seen here on the reverse curves between Largin and St Pinnock viaducts behind No. 6823 *Oakley Grange* and No. 1023 *County of Oxford* on Saturday 4th July 1959. The photograph shows the nature of the curvature and the gradient on this section making heavy work for the firemen. *P. Gray*

St Pinnock was the highest viaduct in Cornwall, 151 feet high and 211 yards in length. It was rebuilt in 1880, the timbered section being replaced by extended masonry work and wrought iron decking. No. 6826 *Nannerth Grange* is seen crossing this notable structure, westward, with the 7.00 am Swindon–Penzance on 4th July 1959. Note again the tremendous scenery to be enjoyed from the train. *P. Gray*

Double-heading again. Here, 4-6-0s Nos. 6931 *Aldborough Hall* and 7820 *Dinmore Manor* are seen crossing Clinnick viaduct, between Bodmin Road and Doublebois with the 10.00 pm Newquay–Paddington on 4th July 1959. This train, formed of a mixture of stock, numbered fifteen coaches making it a hard climb, the gradients here being 1 in 68.   *P. Gray*

the next seven miles to Brownqueen tunnel ran as fierce as 1 in 57 and averaged again at 1 in 70, making this section something of a trial for heavy eastbound trains.

Westwood was the first of the viaducts west of Doublebois. At 124 yards in length and 88 feet high the original structure was replaced in 1879. Westwood quarry, the source of building stone for the viaducts, was alongside and to the south. Less than half a mile further west came St Pinnock viaduct, the highest in Cornwall at 151 feet and 211 yards in length. St Pinnock was rebuilt in 1880, the timbers being replaced by extended masonry work and wrought iron decking. Largin viaduct, at 130 feet in height and 189 yards length, followed at just under half a mile. Like St Pinnock, it was rebuilt with extended masonry sections and iron decking, this being in 1886. Largin signal box, at what must be the most isolated and lonely location on the main line, was opened west of the viaduct on the 'down' side. The box dates from the early years of the century and since 1964 has controlled movements over Largin and St Pinnock viaducts. The line was singled over and between these two viaducts in 1964 to avoid the extensive work required by that time to maintain double track working. The economy of single line operations here has served its purpose through to the present day.

West Largin viaduct, the first to be rebuilt, in 1875, stood on a 1 in 70 gradient. Replaced by a masonry structure, this viaduct was 105 yards long and 75 feet high. Only a quarter of a mile distant again was Draw Wood viaduct, replaced by an embankment and retaining wall, also in 1875. Derrycombe, another viaduct rebuilt in masonry, was another half a mile westward. At 123 yards in length and 77 feet high, this timber structure was replaced in 1881.

The steep descent westward continues, crossing the final two viaducts before Bodmin Road station, now known as Bodmin Parkway. Clinnick viaduct, 110 yards long and 74 feet high, was rebuilt in masonry in 1879, an interesting feature of this particular viaduct being the attractive wrought iron railing. Penadlake viaduct, 142 yards in length and 42 feet high was rebuilt in 1877 and stands nearly three quarters of a mile west of Clinnick and a mile and three quarters east of Bodmin Road. Including the original Draw Wood viaduct there were no less than eight viaducts between Doublebois and Bodmin Road, a distance of almost six miles. This particular section of the main line with its endless curves, numerous viaducts and fierce gradients was doubled from December 1893.

The Glynn Valley clay siding of 1875 and the later, much larger, Newbridge clay dries on the same site should

Above: 'Grange' 4-6-0s Nos. 6832 *Brockton Grange* and 6825 *Llanvair Grange* double-head the 8.15 am Perranporth–Paddington through Bodmin Road on 4th July 1959. The densely wooded and somewhat isolated rural location of Bodmin Road can well be appreciated in this view, as, indeed, can the marked curvature through the station. *P. Gray*

Left: Framed by Bodmin Road's unusual water tower, No. 1006 *County of Cornwall* departs with the 1.55 pm Penzance–Plymouth stopping service on Whit Monday 18th May 1959. The confined area at the 'up' end of the platform made it necessary for the water tower to be positioned like this. Note also the stove to prevent freezing during winter. Together with the water tower, Bodmin Road also once had another interesting feature at the opposite end of the 'up' platform. This was a mirror set on a signal post to allow the signalman an unobstructed view of 'up' trains. The mirror allowed the signalman to have a clear sighting of tail lamps as the trains left on the sharp curve eastward.

M. Mensing

4-6-0 No. 4908 *Broome Hall* leaves Bodmin Road with the 'down' 'Cornishman' on 11th June 1956. The chocolate and cream liveried standard coaching stock was almost new at that time, being introduced that year. The 'Cornish Riviera' of course and the 'Royal Duchy' were the two other named trains with this type of stock.   *M. Mensing*

also be mentioned here, being located 1¼ miles east of Bodmin Road on the down side. Served by pipeline from workings developed by Onslow China Clays Ltd on Bodmin Moor, a considerable distance northward, the Newbridge dries dated from 1931. Onslow Sidings were controlled by their own signalbox, opened in 1931 and closed in 1968 when the site was abandoned.

Bodmin Road, junction for Bodmin General and Wadebridge from May 1887, has been covered in some detail in the chapter on the branch itself. The construction of this branch called for large scale engineering works at the station to extend the site and level the ground for the extra siding accommodation required. Leaving the station, west-bound trains descend at 1 in 65 gradient for half a mile, thereafter making a short climb to pass through Brown-queen tunnel, 88 yards in length.

From Bodmin Road to Lostwithiel the line stays close to the River Fowey and curves to the south following the Fowey Valley. Respryn Bridge, a short distance north-east of Brownqueen tunnel, characterised the extremely attractive landscape of the district where woodland, hillside, fields, meadows and the river combined to their best effect. This location was also of interest historically. Respryn marked the site of a private station serving nearby Lanhydrock House. For a short period in the early summer of 1859 the station at Respryn was also used by public services, this being prior to the completion of Bodmin Road, opened on 26th June.

Beyond Brownqueen tunnel the valley bottom broadens and the descent towards Lostwithiel becomes much easier. To the west, commanding a superb hilltop site, Restormel Castle stands watch over the lush green countryside. The castle also marks the approach to Lostwithiel, where this particular survey of the Great Western main line in East Cornwall ends.

Bodmin Road – 1907

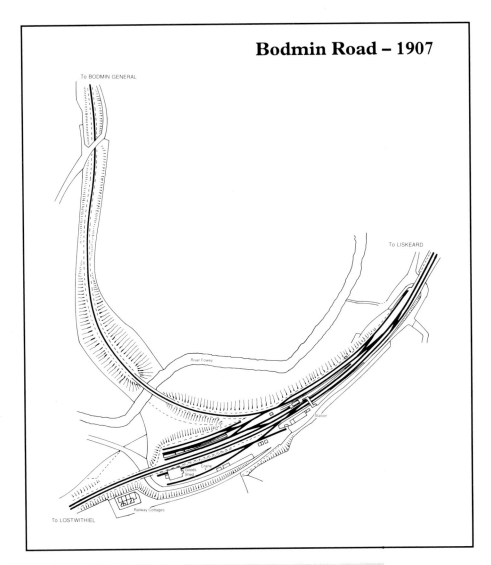

To BODMIN GENERAL

To LISKEARD

River Fowey

Station

Goods Shed

Crane

Railway Cottages

To LOSTWITHIEL

'Castle' class No. 5092 *Tresco Abbey* is seen leaving Bodmin Road with the Manchester–Penzance service on Whit Monday 18th May 1959. The falling gradient, at 1 in 66, is easily seen here, together with the goods shed alongside which, being on level ground, serves to emphasise the descent on the main line.

M. Mensing

Chapter Four

Main Line Deviation: Saltash – St Germans

Under its Act of 11 August 1903 the GWR was authorised to build a deviation line of 4 miles 58 chains from Saltash to St Germans. The new route was needed to replace the old single line section with its five timbered tidal viaducts, opened as part of the original Cornwall Railway in May 1859. Planned to include only three viaducts, the new line enabled the ruling gradient to be reduced from 1 in 62 to 1 in 120 and eased the maximum severity of the curves from 24 to 30 chains. A tunnel was also included in the route. Costs for the construction of this heavily engineered project with its double track and many other improvements were said to be little or no more than the amount required to upgrade the original line.

Work began on 7th March 1904. The Resident Engineer was W.F. Fox, and the contractor R.T. Relf and Son of Plymouth, who also had carried out duties on the construction of the Plymouth, Devonport and South-Western Junction Railway from Plymouth to Lydford.

From the west end of Coombe Lake viaduct at Saltash, rebuilt in 1894, the new line ran parallel with the original as far as Wearde Siding, a distance of 53 chains. Thereafter, the new line took an inland course. A short distance east of

the point of deviation was Defiance Halt, first opened in March 1905. The original halt was on the south side of the line above Wearde Quay and was constructed by crew members of *HMS Defiance*, the torpedo training school nearby. With the opening of the deviation new accommodation was required and the Great Western provided wooden platforms for both 'up' and 'down' lines with corrugated pagoda style shelters and oil lamps. Access to the new platforms was via stairs leading down from an overbridge at the west end of the site; the bridge carried the minor road from Saltash to Wearde Quay. Defiance Platform closed to passengers in October 1930.

Leaving the original route, the new line entered a cutting and then followed along an embankment to reach Forder viaduct. This structure of nine arches was 233 yards long and 69 feet above high water mark. Forder gave passengers the opportunity to enjoy spectacular landscapes north and south of the line. To the north and on the west side of the tidal creek Trematon Castle stood guard over the rolling wooded countryside, looking down on the passing trains. Southward gave fine views over Antony Passage and the Torpoint peninsula beyond; the immediate riverside

No. 6815 *Frilford Grange* with the 7.30 am Penzance–Bristol passes Wearde Quay signalbox on 25th July 1959. This location marks the beginning of the 1908 deviation to St Germans; the train can be seen leaving this alignment which curves away in a cutting to the left beyond the signalbox. Note the water tower tucked into the cutting opposite the signalbox and the water column used by locomotives standing on the loop.

P. Gray

Original route (1859) Saltash – St Germans
Wivelscombe viaduct 1878

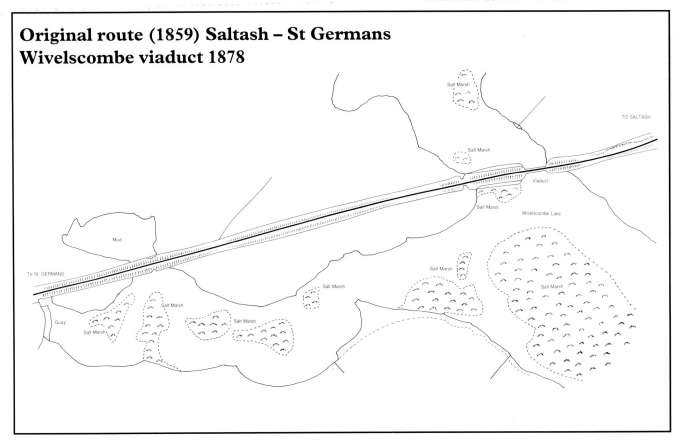

community and quay below the viaduct also added to the interest.

By contrast the line then entered a cutting, 45 feet deep and almost half a mile long. In completing this work it was necessary to remove 136,000 cubic yards of spoil. After a succession of alternate cuttings and embankments came yet further evidence of the heavy engineering which characterised the line. Shillingham tunnel, 452 yards in length, was not easy to build. The approaches from east and west were through deep cuttings which later gave problems with landslips. Large quantities of hard blue elvan rock also had to be removed in tunneling. It was estimated that a workforce of some 700 men were employed at the site with a navvy encampment being located close by. The settlement was known to the navvies as 'Tintown' in view of the temporary corrugated iron accommodation made available. The huts here were each in the charge of a husband and wife who cooked, washed and generally provided board and lodging for about 12 men. Shillingham tunnel was brick lined throughout and was built in horseshoe section. It marked a 1 in 200 gradient falling westward and beyond the western exit was an unusually straight section of track for the Cornish main line.

Running onward over a further embankment the line reached the attractive River Lynher, crossed by means of Notter viaduct. This structure was of eight arches with an overall length of 210 yards. Height above high water was 63 feet. Beyond the viaduct the line was carried through a massive cutting of 24 chains, reaching a depth of 76 feet. Over 210,000 cubic yards of spoil were removed here, much of it going for embankment work east and west of the site. Work at the cuttings was greatly assisted by the services of the 'steam navvy.'

As the line crossed the substantial embankment leading to the River Tiddy and St Germans viaduct it was carried over the original route, some 20 feet higher. St Germans viaduct was the longest and highest on the 1908 deviation. It consisted of 13 arches, was 326 yards long and measured 99 feet from high water to rail level. The foundations here, always difficult given the mud in the tidal creeks, reached down a further 60 feet. When first opened the line was single between Notter and St Germans as the embankment leading to St Germans viaduct was incomplete. A temporary girder bridge provided the important connection until the embankment was ready.

The line opened on Sunday 22nd March 1908. At daybreak, in heavy rain, two gangs of men were brought to Wearde Siding and to St Germans. Lengths of rail ready secured to sleepers were on site to make for rapid connections at each end. From 6.30 am to 10.00 am the engineers had possession of the 'up' line from Wearde Siding to Saltash. The single section remained in use until 10.08 am when it was also cut and re-connected for the new route. The last 'down' train to use the old route was the 9.15 am from Plymouth; the last 'up' train was the 9.55 am from St Germans. Following this, the engineers took complete possession of the line, but single working was available over the new route by 11.15 am. The Engineers' train of one locomotive and a coach worked over the line and was followed by normal services using a single line. Double track working was introduced by the evening between Saltash and Notter.

At St Germans the original timber viaduct stood just to the north of its replacement, which meant that with the new line it was both necessary and to the general advantage to realign the track, giving an easier curve at the east end of the station, bringing the main line southward.

Sections of the original route at the east end of the new deviation were retained. One was the length from the junction with the new line at the new Wearde signalbox (1908) westward almost to the creek and the site of the original

34

Forder viaduct. The two lengths of sidings here provided useful accommodation for empty stock. Eastward from Wearde signalbox, on the south side, part of the original main line was also used as a 'down' refuge siding running behind Defiance Platform. During World War Two this refuge siding was converted to a down goods loop, extended eastward to a point just west of Coombe Lake viaduct, Saltash.

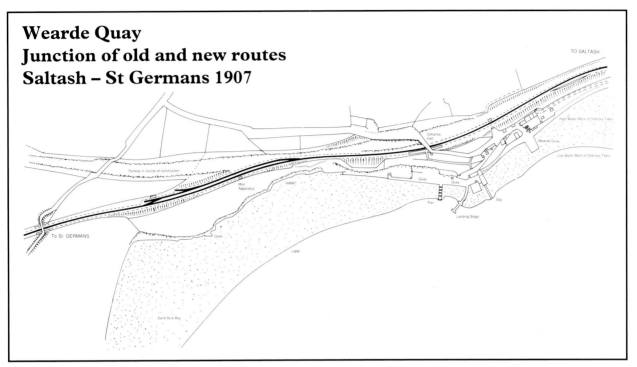

Wearde Quay
Junction of old and new routes
Saltash – St Germans 1907

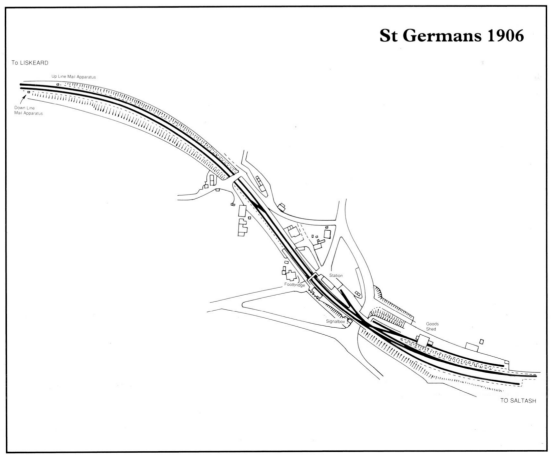

St Germans 1906

A great sense of occasion, well recorded. The scene at Saltash at the official opening of the Royal Albert Bridge on the Cornwall Railway, 2nd May 1859. Welcomed and cheered by the local community, the Prince Consort is shown here leaving the train in order to inspect the bridge. Note the station buildings, the flags decorating the bridge, and the guard of honour, standing amongst the crowds on both platforms.   *Penzance Library*

Having fulfilled his duty in officially opening the bridge and giving it its name, Prince Albert departed on board the steamer *Vivid*. The vessel is shown here beneath the bridge with a large crowd gathered to witness the departure.   *Penzance Library*

Chapter Five
Saltash

As the railway's gateway to and from the county of Cornwall, Saltash occupied an important position on the main line. This enabled the town to develop in itself whilst it also encouraged growth in the surrounding rural districts.

The Royal Cornwall Gazette drew attention to growth in the town, linked with railway activity and the construction of the Royal Albert Bridge.

From that date (1853) the revival of the prosperity of Saltash may be dated, since which the numerous tokens of improvement set forth every year augur happily for its future fortunes – numerous houses and villas being erected in its vicinity, a system of drainage adopted; two lines of steamers started and commodious landing stages erected.

Kelly's Directory also drew attention to fashionable development that gradually characterised the town.

Port View, where many good houses have been erected, is regarded as one of the most beautiful localities in the West of England.

The summer regatta and steamer trips on the river contributed towards a stylish image whilst the twice yearly cattle shows underlined the role of the busy market centre.

Prior to the opening of the Plymouth, Devonport and South Western Junction Railway in June 1890 and of the Callington – Bere Alston line of March 1908, Saltash handled much of the fruit and flower traffic of the Tamar Valley. *The West Briton* of 23rd June 1870 reported the development of traffic in strawberries:

The greatly increased facilities afforded by the railway transit have given an immense impetus to the cultivation of this delicious fruit in the neighbourhood of Gunnislake and Calstock during the past few years, the quantity grown this year being considerably more than hitherto. By far the greater portion is sent to the London markets, but no insignificant quantity finds its way as far north as Glasgow. The stations from which the fruit is sent are Tavistock and Saltash. From the former alone nearly 30 tons have been despatched since the commencement of the season and the cost of carriage of

Saltash in more prosperous, positive days. This view, taken from the 'down' platform looking towards the Royal Albert Bridge, shows an extremely well maintained station reflecting the high standards of the GWR in the inter-war years. The photograph, whilst giving full details of station layout, also testifies to an appealing sense of order and purpose, stability and confidence.

Cornwall Local Studies Library

Saltash station in busier days. The well kept appearance and the tidy bookstall indicates a busy and important location. Saltash saw a lot of suburban traffic to and from Plymouth prior to the opening of the Tamar road bridge in 1961. The 2.10 pm auto train stands on the 'up' platform preparing to leave for Plymouth. Saltash station was rebuilt in 1880 with extensions and modifications also taking place in 1908. 2nd January 1960.

P. Gray

a single night's consignment will sometimes amount to £16. The night mail trains now emit a most delightful perfume, which contrasts in a most agreeable manner with the unpleasant odour from the fish vans.

In the previous year the same newspaper also drew attention to the districts reputation for cherry crops, which also provided valuable traffic for the railway.

The cherry season is now rapidly approaching and the parishes on the banks of the Tamar – Botusfleming, Calstock, etc. are looking forward to a good crop of the black cherry, or as it is more familiarly known, 'mazzards'. One grower alone has advertised for thirty men to gather cherries – The same grower guarantees to supply fruit dealers with 30 cwt daily during the season.

At the Half-Yearly meeting of the Cornwall Railway Company in August 1880 direct reference was made to the new goods shed and extra siding accommodation recently completed at Saltash. This was essential given the large amounts of garden and agricultural produce passing through, the station. It was also pointed out that passenger traffic had much outgrown the capacity of the station to deal with it and plans for a new station were well underway.

By the turn of the century strawberries were the most important local crop with between 200 and 300 tons being gathered during the season. Raspberries were considered second most important with between 100 and 150 tons being moved. (Women and children working the fields received 3 shillings a day for their labour; the men earned 4

shillings.) Tomatoes were, likewise, under cultivation, being grown on some scale, whilst milk traffic also developed at the station. The entire district westward from Saltash to Lostwithiel was recognised as an important dairying area contributing substantially to the local economy. Other branches of agriculture were also well regarded by the GWR. In March 1936, for example, the Company introduced a country lorry service centring on St Germans station. Grain, fertilisers, feedstuffs, flour, perishables etc. was delivered and collected 'to farms and premises' in the area covering Crafthole, Downderry, Hessenford, Polbathic, Seaton, Tideford and Trerulefoot.

In the Tamar Valley the flower trade eventually assumed prime position with its very success causing problems locally. Just as the fishing communities objected to the handling of fish on Sundays, so, also, did the growers in the Calstock district. In February 1937 the flower growers of Calstock protested vigorously against the Southern Railway's practice of handling traffic on Sundays. Many threatened to withdraw their business from Calstock and the Southern line and send it instead by Great Western services. In view of the fact that in the previous season, 1936, over 200,000 boxes of flowers and over 300 baskets of fruit had been handled, with some 2,000 boxes of anemones being sent away weekly, it represented valuable trade which the GWR would be keen to grasp.

Together with North Cornwall, the Tamar Valley was one of the few parts of Cornwall where the GWR did not enjoy a monopoly of trade, but attempts had been made to open up the area to the GWR. An Act was passed in July 1865 authorising the construction of the Saltash and Callington Railway. This was to be a broad gauge line intended to link with the neighbouring Tamar, Kit Hill and Callington Railway. In the official description it read as follows:

A Railway commencing in the Parish of St Stephen by Saltash by a Junction with the Cornwall Railway at or near Saltash station thereof and terminating in the Parish of Callington at or near the proposed Termination of the Tamar, Kit Hill and Callington Railway.

Access over the latter line was to be by means of the mixed gauge but, in the event, neither line materialised. Callington did get its link to the Tamar, however, initially by the 3 foot 6 inch gauge East Cornwall Minerals Railway of May 1872, and, eventually, by the standard gauge line across the Tamar to Bere Alston in 1908, (Plymouth Devonport and South West Junction Railway) giving access to the LSWR system. A further attempt was made to link Saltash and Callington in 1899, but this also failed. The GWR did however, introduce an omnibus service between Albaston, Callington and Saltash beginning on 1st June 1904, this being a replacement for a coach service dating from May 1876.

Having considered something of the development of Saltash as a town itself and as a market centre for the surrounding area it is also important to consider the growth of links across the Tamar.

The railway offered easy access to and from Plymouth and Devonport, which together had been described by the late 1860s as 'the great emporium and metropolis of the West of England.' Apart from general trade and commerce, the dockyards in particular provided employment opportunities for the people of Saltash and the origins of an early type of suburban service can be traced back to the 1870s.

It was not until the turn of the century, in July 1904, that an intensive service began between Plympton and Saltash. Numerous halts in the Plymouth district were opened as part of the new service, intended to compete with the rival tramways operating between Devonport and Saltash Passage, where they connected with the steam ferries. An intensive suburban rail service, something most unusual for the West Country, brought Saltash into a much closer relationship with the community east of the Tamar. Steam rail motor units worked the new service, which by 1905 consisted of 34 trains in each direction on weekdays and 13 on Sundays.

The 'up' platform at Saltash was extended westward for 1908 and a new steel overbridge replaced the stone structure carrying road traffic over the station. The approach to the Royal Albert Bridge was also improved with two of the wrought iron spans at the western end being replaced. An attractive footbridge was also provided, linking the platforms. Auto train workings soon augmented the rail motors in view of the increase in traffic, the auto trains being able to handle as many as four trailers when required. By the early 1930s the suburban service to and from Saltash was only slightly below 50 trains daily on weekdays with 20 on Sundays.

From 1930 the suburban trains between Plympton and Plymouth were replaced by Western National bus services. The Saltash suburban timetable by 1959 listed 36 weekday services to and from Plymouth with just over 20 on Sundays. Regular steam auto trains workings ended in June 1961, but they still turned out on occasions as substitutes for the new DMU services, as they did also on the local workings between Plymouth and Liskeard. The opening of the Tamar road bridge in 1961 brought the inevitable decline of the local rail service. By 1969 the service had in many ways become part of the Plymouth-Liskeard stopping train timetable, with Saltash reduced to a service of only 15 trains in each direction on weekdays, and no trains at all on Sundays.

The community had grown rapidly during the second half of the nineteenth century, with a population of 3,357 by 1901. Thereafter it was only during the 1920s that it failed to show any increase. In 1921 the population for the Municipal Borough was 6,558 and by 1931 stood at 6,330. Surveys of the following years, however, reflect considerable growth. During the 1930s Saltash Borough grew by 10.6 per cent, whilst the increase for the subsequent period to 1948 was 9.4 per cent. By contrast, the neighbouring Urban District of Torpoint declined by 6.6 per cent in the 1930s and showed an increase of only 0.5 per cent to 1948.

The long term result of the growth in population with the widespread influence of the railway had an impact on the character of the town. Whilst Saltash maintained its role as a market centre for the livestock and for perishable traffic from the surrounding area the town had also been gradually and inevitably drawn into much closer links with Plymouth. In social and economic term Saltash increasingly became a suburb of Plymouth, and with the improved access since 1961 via the Tamar road bridge this process has accelerated.

Chapter Six
The Caradon and Looe Lines

Much to the satisfaction of the local population, *The West Briton* of 6th December 1844 carried the following statement:

> On Thursday, the 28 ultimo, five miles of the railroad which has been in the course of construction for some time, from the Cheesewring to the Liskeard Canal – was opened for the accommodation of the adventurers.
>
> A long train started from the upper terminus and arrived safely at the present completion of the line, where the party was entertained by partaking of a dejeuner, the workmen employed were also regaled with roast beef and strong beer.

The 'adventurers' included leading local business interests of the Liskeard district, and, of course, the principal shareholders of the Caradon Mines and the Liskeard and Looe Union Canal Company. With the extensive deposits of the Caradon copper mines yielding rich prizes application had been made to Parliament to build a rail link from the workings on Caradon Hill to the canal basin at Moorswater. The canal had been in operation since March 1828. Under an Act of 26 June 1843, the Liskeard and Caradon Railway was empowered to build a line of almost 6½ miles, with extensions to Tokenbury Corner and the granite quarries at the Cheesewring, the latter involving the 1 in 11 rope-worked Gonamena Incline. Capital amounted to £12,000 in £25 shares with powers to borrow a further £4,000. The newspaper report, here, covered the celebrations for the partial opening of the line to Tremabe, some three miles short of the canal basin at Moorswater. The Company had to wait until March 1846 to see the line completed.

Given the local geography, the line was characterised by severe curves and a ruling gradient of 1 in 60 to lift it on to Caradon Hill. It was built to the standard gauge 4' 8½" with rails set on granite sleeper blocks, these being easily obtained from the quarries nearby. Horses were used to haul the wagons upward from Moorswater, with loaded trucks being worked downward by gravity, and controlled by a brakesman. Charges by the mid 1850s were given as follows: 'Ores, coals, bricks etc. 4d per ton per mile; Lime, limestone, culm, manure, granite, slate, 2d per ton per mile; Corn, potatoes, hay, cattle, salt, 6d per ton per mile.'

Copper mining at Caradon began relatively late by Cornish standards. Whereas the mines further west had often been worked from the mid to late eighteenth century, development at Caradon dated from the 1830s. The quality and extent of the ore, however, encouraged rapid expansion. By 1844, for example, 410 people were employed at South Caradon Mine alone; eleven years later the numbers had increased to more than 600. Over its full period of production 1837-1885 this mine produced 217,820 tons of copper ore. Other important workings within the district included Marke Valley, north east of Caradon Hill, producing 128,500 tons of ore between 1844-1890, and West Caradon and Phoenix United, producing 82,690 and 91,700 tons respectively in the overall period 1843-1887.

Quarrying also became important within the district. The moorlands north of Caradon Hill provided the Cheesewring Granite Company with an abundance of excellent quality stone, much in demand for major building works in many parts of Britain. Looking to extend their interests the Granite company opened new quarries at Kilmar Tor some 1½ miles north of the Cheesewring from 1856. These workings were extremely isolated and the Company planned a line across the moorland to serve their quarries. The Granite company built its line to the standard gauge with rails set onto granite sleeper blocks. The opening took place on 26th August 1858 with *The Royal Cornwall Gazette* reporting the event:

> About 10.30 (am) a number of the waggons decorated with flags and evergreens started from the Moorswater terminus conveying the directors and shareholders with many of their friends, and arrived at Kilmar about 2 o'clock, where a collation was spread in a tent to which they did ample justice. There was also a spread out of doors for the workmen and others. After dinner a number of toasts were given and responded to. A tea was also provided for the persons employed at the granite works at the Cheesewring, after which the train started for Moorswater, and arrived there without any accident

Guard Uren stands for the camera whilst working a train at Moorswater. This sturdy and resolute member of staff is wearing the uniform of the Liskeard and Caradon Company. Note the condition of the platform with its rough timbering.

Cornwall Local Studies Library, Redruth

about 7 o'clock, all being much pleased with the day's excursion.

Amongst the more well known projects to use granite from these quarries was the Thames Embankment work, and the extensive coastal defences at Portsmouth and Plymouth after 1860. Development from 1860 of Glasgow Caradon Consols mining sett east of the South Caradon workings also underlined the need for the other railway extensions, this time, eastward from Crows Nest to Tokenbury. Powers to build this section of line were gained through the Liskeard and Caradon Railway Act of May 1860.

Somewhat earlier, on 4th May 1844, *The Mining Journal* drew attention to the tremendous changes visited upon the Caradon district with the rapid development of mining and quarrying. In keeping with what for many contemporaries was almost an article of faith, the spread of industrial activity was equated with unquestioned progress and was celebrated accordingly.

> The change which the hand of science has effected here is a subject of great congratulation; the moors in the parish of St Cleer, barren and desolate in the extreme on which nothing useful to the purposes of man was found, but huge masses of granite or scanty sheep pasture, and which were as silent as they were desolate, have assumed a cheerfulness and activity, the result of noisy and busy labour.

With such great potential here in the mines and quarries came the need, by the mid century, for improved access to the sea at Looe. The canal, whose earlier traffic had been largely agricultural, was increasingly under pressure and a railway was considered essential. On 11th May 1858 the Bill for the canal company's Liskeard and Looe line passed through Parliament. Finances amounted to £13,000 in £25 shares. Silvanus Jenkin was appointed Engineer, the contract for the line going to John Brown and William Williams, whilst Messrs Bone, Firks and Sargeant took the contract for the bridges. By March 1859 *The Cornish Times* reported that the rails for the whole line (supplied by the Rhymney Iron Company) had been purchased, and that agreements with the local landowners, and with the Duchy for use of the foreshore at Looe, had been reached. The section of line from Moorswater to Tregarland, the latter just north of Sandplace, was laid on granite blocks; to the south the track was set on wooden sleepers.

The line opened to traffic on 27th December 1860. It ran through the parishes of Liskeard, St Keyne, Morval, Duloe and St Martins by Looe. Construction was not difficult in view of the river valley route alongside the canal, but several bridges were needed at various points to allow roads, the canal and the river to cross the line. Motive power for the early freight traffic came in the form of an 0-6-0 tank engine named *Liskeard*. Built at Newport, it was brought to Liskeard on 26th December 1860 via the Cornwall Railway and was then transported to Moorswater with the assistance of a team of 28 horses.

Details of the opening ceremony were given by *The Royal Cornwall Gazette*:

> The proceedings of Thursday were very successful. The opening train consisting of a locomotive engine and 12 open trucks started from Moorswater amidst the cheers of numerous spectators shortly after half past ten. It contained the directors, several of the gentlemen of the neighbourhood, the band of the Liskeard Rifle Corps and many of the members, besides a host of other persons.
>
> At every little village and hamlet through which the train passed, the cottagers came out and cheered lustily, and in one or two places triumphal arches of more or less beauty were erected, under which the train had to pass. At a few minutes after 11 am it arrived at the terminus in East Looe, which at present is on the extensive quay running by the side of the harbour, commencing from the bridge.
>
> At Looe everyone turned out and did their best to welcome the train. The streets were gaily decorated and arches of evergreens erected in great variety, with all kinds of appropriate mottos.

The train was met by the Mayor and Corporation and the entire gathering then proceeded to the Town Hall for further ceremonial and the enjoyment of a public dinner. The speeches that followed paid tribute to the railway. In one instance it was said that, had it not been for the railway, the town of Looe would have gone back to a position of 30 years previous, as a mere fishing port. Progress and prosperity had visited Looe. By way of illustration and analogy it was emphasised that, 'as Athens had its Piraeus, Manchester its Liverpool, Liskeard might now have its Looe'. Looe was considered to be only in its infancy.

Together with the arrival of the railway, there were other significant pointers to progress at Looe. The Looe Harbour Commissioners were formed in 1848 to oversee improvements at the port, their main work, initially, being the construction of a breakwater and the provision of new quays. Work was slow, however, for lack of finance particularly in the early stages. The local community derived great benefit, however, from the new bridge opened in 1855 linking East and West Looe, whilst the church was restored and enlarged over the period 1852-1862. A new market house was opened in 1853, a gas works in 1866 and the Guildhall in 1877.

In the same year that the railway opened from Moorswater to Looe (1860) the Caradon Railway progressed with their plans to introduce steam power on the line and to upgrade it accordingly. The Liskeard and Caradon Railway Act of 15th May 1860 opened the way to such improvements, including also the construction of the Tokenbury branch and the purchase of the Kilmar Railway, opened in August 1858. An agreement was made between the Liskeard and Caradon and the canal company in 1862 with reference to the working of their lines, bringing a new level of cooperation. The Caradon company worked the lines and eventually, in January 1878, leased the Canal Company's line.

Steam power became an important feature on the two lines from 1862 with the arrival of the 0-6-0 saddle tank, *Caradon* built by Gilkes, Wilson and Co of Middlesbrough. Two years later a second saddle tank, *Cheesewring* was also purchased from the Middlesbrough company. This locomotive, another 0-6-0, was eventually taken into Great Western stock, being numbered 1311. August 1866 saw the end of *Liskeard's* working life on the line, the locomotive being sold elsewhere. A further locomotive, *Kilmar* was purchased in 1869. With detailed modifications it survived into Great Western ownership as number 1312. Two further

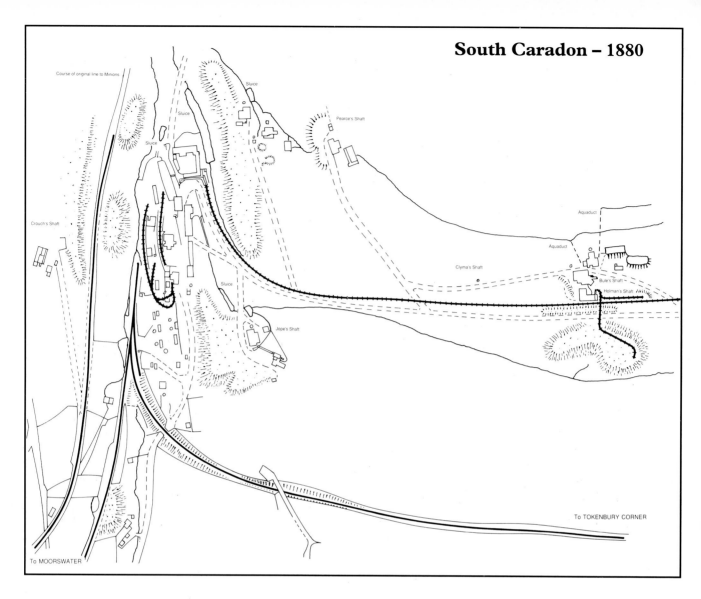

locomotives of 1901 and 1902 were the 0-6-0 saddle tank *Looe*, and the well known 2-4-0 tank *Lady Margaret* remained at work until shortly after World War One when it was transferred to the Cambrian Railway. This locomotive carried the GWR Number 1308, and survived until 1948.

Passenger services between Moorswater and Looe began on 11th September 1879, following a satisfactory inspection by the Board of Trade five days earlier. Two trains in each direction made up the weekday service, with an extra working each way on Saturdays.

T/T 1880	1/2	1/2/3	Sats only
Moorswater	9-45	4-00	7-10
Causeland	10-00	4-15	7-24
Looe	10-17	4-32	7-42
Looe	10-45	5-35	7-50
Causeland	11-06	5-52	8-07
Moorswater	11-20	6-05	8-22

Causeland was the only intermediate station at that date, with Sandplace following in December 1881 and St Keyne in October 1902.

The Board of Trade refused the Liskeard and Caradon permission to introduce passenger services above Moorswater in 1882. The severe curvature and condition of the line generally being given as reasons for the refusal. Despite this, passengers were carried on an unofficial basis using open wagons. Details of special excursion traffic were given in the local press, such as the following from *The Cornish Times* of 16 September 1882.

On Monday, 25th September, a train will run from Rillaton Bridge, Cheesewring, to Looe and back, leaving Rillaton Bridge 8.30 am, Tokenbury Corner 8.40; Railway Terrace 9.00; St Clear 9.10; Liskeard 9.52; returning from Looe at 5.30 pm. Tickets for the double journey 1 shilling if purchased on or before Friday 22nd September, after this date 1 shilling and 3 pence. Children half-price. Proceeds to be devoted to reduction of debt on Minions Chapel –.

The extension of the line from Tokenbury Corner around Caradon Hill to Minions was completed in November 1877 giving much improved access to the Cheesewring Quarries and Phoenix Mine. This allowed for the closure of the Gonamena Incline. Further plans to extend the system also followed soon after. In 1884 the Company obtained an Act to continue its line northward across the bleak moorland to make a junction with the London and South Western Railway's North Cornwall Line. Work began on this extension that year but the

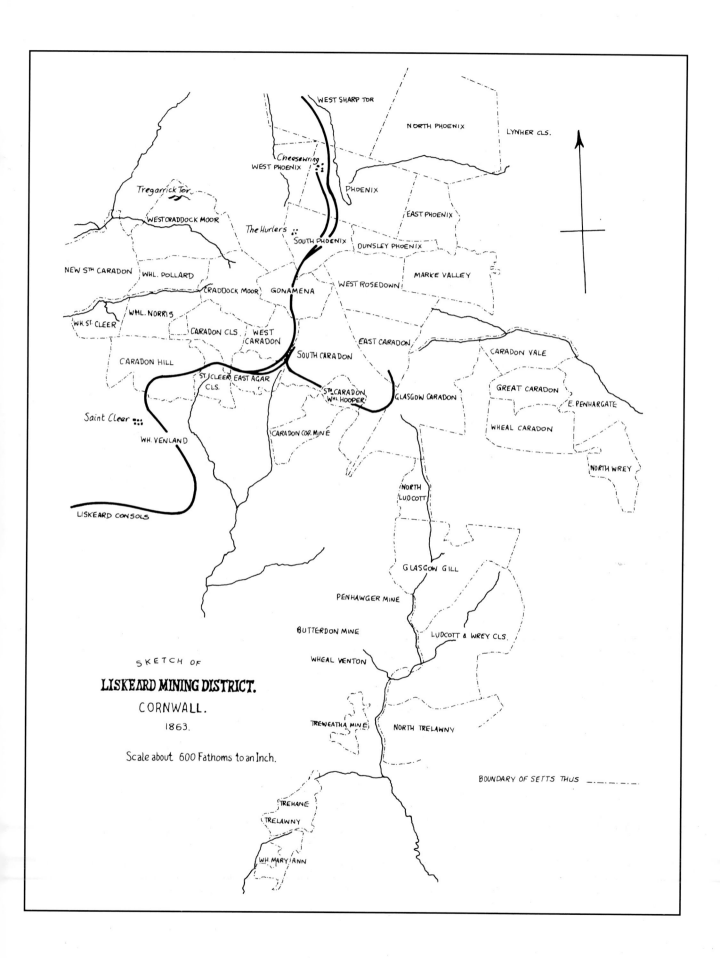

WEST SHARP TOR

NORTH PHOENIX

LYNHER CLS.

Cheesewring
WEST PHOENIX

Tregarrick Tor

Phoenix

WESTCRADDOCK MOOR

EAST PHOENIX

The Hurlers
SOUTH PHOENIX

DUNSLEY PHOENIX

NEW Sᵀᴴ CARADON

WHL. POLLARD

MARKE VALLEY

CRADDOCK MOOR
GONAMENA

WEST ROSEDOWN

WHL. NORRIS

WH. Sᵀ. CLEER

CARADON CLS.
WEST
CARADON

EAST CARADON

CARADON VALE

CARADON HILL

South Caradon

GREAT CARADON

Sᵀ. CLEER EAST AGAR
CLS.

Sᵀᴴ. CARADON
WHL HOOPER

GLASGOW CARADON

E. PENHARGATE

Saint Cleer

WHEAL CARADON

WH. VENLAND

CARADON COR. MINE

NORTH WREY

LISKEARD CONSOLS

NORTH
LUDCOTT

GLASGOW GILL

PENHAWGER MINE

BUTTERDON MINE

LUDCOTT & WREY CLS.

WHEAL VENTON

SKETCH OF

LISKEARD MINING DISTRICT.

CORNWALL.

1863.

Scale about 600 Fathoms to an Inch.

TREWEATHA MINE

NORTH TRELAWNY

BOUNDARY OF SETTS THUS ___ . ___ . ___

TREHANE

TRELAWNY

WH. MARY ANN

'4575' class No. 5557 and brake van stand outside the Liskeard and Caradon locomotive shed at Moorswater on 15th March 1960. The original route northward to the Caradon district ran alongside the shed as shown here, but this section serving the mines and quarries was lifted in 1917. Moorswater shed closed in September 1960. 4th July 1959. *P. Gray*

collapse of the copper market proved disastrous for South Caradon and the other mines of the district. South Caradon closed in 1885 depriving the line of a great deal of revenue both in ore traffic to Looe, and coal together with mining equipment and supplies previously carried up to Caradon. Without the benefit of South Caradon's pumping engines the neighbouring mines were also put into extreme difficulties with flood water. The closure of the Caradon mines inevitably meant the end of all plans to extend northward, and 1886 also saw the appointment of a Receiver to handle the company's affairs underlining the rapid decline in fortunes.

Tourism offered some degree of consolation. The ailing local economy so closely bound to mining and its associated engineering interests was gradually assisted by the growing tourist market. Looe, like many other locations around the Cornish coast, was included in publications such as the 1904 *Seaside Watering Places*. Putting emphasis upon the natural beauty of the coastline and the attraction of a healthy environment, this particular publication presented a very positive view of the town.

A stone bridge arches over the river, the latter dividing just above into two branches, which run a very serpentine course between hills covered with beautiful hanging woods, reminding one vividly of the Lake District. The air is remarkably soft, and invalids, more especially those suffering from chest infections, drawing great benefit from a sojourn here. The beaches at East and West Looe are well adapted for bathing. There are several bathing machines and the shoal water makes bathing so safe that a fatality in this connection has not occurred from the beaches for the last forty years. –

A new road has been cut to the Hannafore West Building Estate, and a splendid marine drive along the seafront is thus obtained. Several villas have been built and others are in preparation. There is a good lawn tennis ground on the common at West Looe from which a lovely view of the sea and surrounding countryside can be obtained. West Looe has a good water supply and system of drainage; and at East Looe an additional supply of water is being brought in –

Neat and tidy lodgings are to be had at East and West Looe, and at Polperro, and there are a few comfortable hotels. Only increased accommodation is wanted to make this sheltered watering place rival some of the more obtrusive seaside resorts.

Given the provision for increased accommodation, the publicity to follow from the GWR, and the convenience of a direct rail link to the Cornish main line at Liskeard, Looe was well placed to grow as an attractive resort.

Chapter Seven

The Link Line: Coombe Junction – Liskeard

The earliest attempt to link the Caradon lines with the Cornwall Railway main line dated from 1846. Under the Cornwall Railway Act of that year provision was made to lease or purchase the Caradon lines and make a direct connection. This failed to materialise because of the acute financial problems faced by the Cornwall Railway, but in later years further schemes were put forward attempting the link. These included the construction of a rack railway from Moorswater to Liskeard, on a gradient of 1 in 7; a plan for a hydraulic hoist, also at Moorswater, and proposals in 1892 for a conventional railway.

A successful scheme, however, had to wait until 1895. In that year Joseph Thomas, a respected engineer well known to the district, put forward a plan, finally accepted, to build a line from a junction at Coombe, south of Moorswater, to the Cornwall Railway (GWR) station, climbing the Liskeard Valley.

A railway one mile seven furlongs and three chains or thereabouts in length, commencing by a junction with the railway of the Company (ie the Union Canal Company) and terminating in a south-easterly direction from the main entrance to the booking office of the Great Western Railway Company Liskeard Station.

The proposals for this Liskeard and Looe Extension Railway were duly presented to Parliament, gaining the Royal Assent on 6th July 1895. Joseph Thomas was engineer to the line; the contractor being J.C. Lang of Liskeard, well known for work on the Cornwall Railway. With capital of £30,000 and powers to borrow a further £10,000 the Liskeard and Looe Railway Company (now officially recognised as a railway, not a canal undertaking) was also empowered to repossess its line from the Caradon company and acquire the latter's locomotives and rolling stock by compulsory purchase.

A 'Grange' takes a fairly long freight train westward across Liskeard viaduct on Sunday 6th August 1961. The photograph was taken from the track bed of the 1901 link line dropping down from Liskeard to Coombe Junction and from this distance the train has the appearance of a model. Liskeard parish church can be seen in the far background. *P. Gray*

A beautiful study of rural England showing just how well the railway formed part of the landscape. On a magnificently hot Sunday afternoon in early August 1961. '4500' class 2-6-2T No. 4574 drops down the gradient from Liskeard to Coombe Junction. Bolitho viaduct carrying the main line can be seen amidst the fields in the background.   *P. Gray*

Financial problems then brought the plan to a halt. Local capital was insufficient and the Company sought the interest of the GWR but without success. The Great Western welcomed the prospect of the new line but felt themselves unable to take it on because of conflict between the two existing companies – Caradon and Looe – together with the fact that a great deal of money would be required to bring both these lines up to GWR operating standards. The Liskeard and Looe and Liskeard and Caradon companies were to become involved in litigation over the question of the latter's stock, and its transfer to the Liskeard and Looe. Following legal action in the High Court the transfer was finalised only on 7th May 1901, when the Receiver handed over the stock to the Secretary of the Liskeard and Looe for services the next day. Also, with reference to GWR reservations about operating standards, it should be noted that in part the track still rested on granite sleeper blocks, Thomas also contacted the Westminster firm of Messrs Chambers and Son to get them to make an inspection of the line with a view to financial backing. They declined on the grounds that the project showed insufficient stock for their direct interest.

The project was finally rescued by one Captain J.E.P. Spicer of Spye Park, Chippenham. Spicer, with other interested parties, bought some £20,000 worth of stock thus becoming the main-spring of development, with, of course, thanks to Joseph Thomas for good services in promoting the line.

With nothing now to delay proceedings, Sylvanus Jenkin, Senior Engineer to the earlier Looe Railway, cut the first sod on 28th June 1898, to get work underway. Although only ¾ mile apart as the crow flies, Moorswater and Liskeard were separated by an extremely steep slope. Coombe is 130 feet above sea level whilst Liskeard station stands on the hill 335 feet above sea level. To overcome this the line made an elliptical climb, utilising the slopes of the Liskeard Valley.

At Coombe the canal had to be diverted, with the original cut being filled in for some distance to carry the new line. A short distance south of Coombe Junction signalbox and the level crossing, giving access from the road to Coombe House, the new route turned away from the Looe line climbing on an embankment and crossing Coombe Lane on a masonry bridge. It continued through a plantation, to pass under the Liskeard – Looe highway at Lodge Hill. Here the line turns on a 10½ chain curve from a south-east to a north-easterly direction and passes through Lodge Hill cutting. This was to be one of the deepest cuttings in the county, being driven through solid rock. Lodge Hill took two years four months to complete. Work

'4500' class 2-6-2T No. 4508 begins its climb, largely at 1m 40, from Coombe Junction to Liskeard. The Looe line runs down the valley to the left of the train, whilst Coome Junction box and one of the arches of the main line Moorswater viaduct add further railway interest to this magnificently rural setting. 10th July 1955.   *R.C. Riley*

started here on 1st August 1898, the same day as construction commenced on the Heathlands Lane and Gut Hill cuttings at Liskeard. The foreman in charge of these works was James Bidgood. One workman died at Lodge Hill during the course of construction, the result of a rock fall.

Following its course into the Liskeard Valley the line climbed at gradients of 1 in 40 and was to run along its eastern slopes, passing beneath Liskeard viaduct, between the second and third piers. The embankment beneath the main line viaduct was made wider than originally intended because of a landslip at Bolitho cutting. The spoil from the slip, estimated at 5,000 cubic yards, was used on the embankment as extra support. Indeed, the technique of construction with the alternate cuttings and embankments, the spoil from the former being used for the latter, was hailed as 'the chief engineering merit of the line.'

Bolitho cutting followed. It was begun on 1st October 1898 and completed on 9th August 1899. This was on the straight section on the valley's eastern slope and, as mentioned, suffered the landslip; the wet weather causing the grassy clay bed to give way. Bolitho cutting was followed by the remarkably sharp curve of 8 chains taking the line round on no less than a 270° turn across the Liskeard Valley to the western slope. Given the severity of this curve, the Lodge Hill 10½ chain achievement was, by comparison, described as 'comparatively trifling forming an arc of only 90°'. The line here climbs on a gradient of 1 in 60 with a succession of alternate embankments and cutting for this final section on the approach to Liskeard station, where the gradient eventually eases to 1 in 200. Gut Lane and Heathlands Lane cuttings were part of the final stretch into and along the western side of the valley. Gut Lane was completed on 9th August 1900, and Heathlands Lane five weeks earlier on 4th July 1900. Figures given for earthworks generally show the movement of 100,000 cubic yards for the cuttings and 192,000 cubic yards for the embankments.

The view from Coombe Junction signalbox looking northward towards the station with Moorswater viaduct in the background. '4500' class 2-6-2T No. 4559 is seen leaving the platform with a train for Liskeard. The single line passing beneath the road bridge led on to the clay dries at Moorswater, a short distance beyond the viaduct. Coombe Junction box was closed in 1981 and the point work is now operated by a ground frame.   *P. Gray*

2-6-2T No. 4552 shunting clay wagons at Moorswater.   *R.C. Riley*

No. 4552 on a freight train from Moorswater to Liskeard on 18th July 1960.   *R.C. Riley*

The Liskeard and Looe terminus was at the east end of the GWR station on the 'up' side, and stood at right angles to the main line platforms. One main building was provided incorporating the booking hall, stationmaster's office, parcels office, general and ladies waiting rooms. Described as well built and commodious the building was constructed of stone and wood and was 202 feet long. The waiting room, like the entire site, was gas-lit, whilst the furnishings included a table and three benches of English oak. Work began on the station in May 1899. Beyond the platform to the west was the signal box and water tower. The goods yard, alongside the station, to the east of the run-round loop, was particularly spacious, being the largest in the county, with the exception of Truro. Access to and from the GWR lines was via the goods yard with the connecting line running from the yard to face westward on the main line. This access was controlled from the GWR signalbox. The four sidings in the yard together with their shunting spur were well planned to handle traffic. Nearest the station was the siding serving the goods platform with ample space immediately east of it for horse drawn traffic, wagons and carts to load and unload. Beyond this roadway were the other lines, one to give through access to the GWR and the two others to handle traffic, separately, to and from the GWR line.

At Coombe, the only crossing place on the line, a new station was provided for the opening services. It was a single sided structure on the east side of the line with a shelter on the platform. Lighting was by oil lamp. Moorswater station, further north immediately beyond Moorswater viaduct, (GWR) was closed on 15th May 1901 when the new station and new line were officially brought into use.

The local press reported trial runs from Coombe to Liskeard on Wednesday and Thursday 27th and 28th February which were considered a complete success. On Friday 1st March Colonel York inspected the line on behalf of the Board of Trade.

Passenger services began over the new route on Wednesday 8th May 1901. Using stock from the Caradon company, the first train left Looe at 8.35 am amidst cheers of a considerable concourse. It was apparently well met at Liskeard, where it steamed into the station at 9.10 am. All trains that day were said to be well patronised, particularly the 2.20 pm from Liskeard. Official celebrations to mark the opening of the line and the link with the railways beyond were arranged for the following week, on the 15th May.

The local population turned out in great numbers to witness the official opening. On the line itself the main train of the day was, without doubt, the Directors Special, departing Liskeard at 1 pm, and carrying, amongst others, the Directors of the Railway, the Mayor of Liskeard, Mr Thomas, Engineer Mr Holbrook, the Traffic Manager and Mr Lang, the contractor. Brilliant weather favoured the proceedings and the departure of the train, formed of the 'new carriages on the American central corridor principle,' headed by the locomotive *Looe*, was marked by sixteen detonators placed on the line. The train arrived at Looe to a spirited welcome from the community in general and from the Urban District Council, the Harbour Commissioners, and the School Board, in particular.

Every vantage point was taken to enjoy the celebrations which, on the arrival of the train, continued with a formal procession to the town and the Guildhall. Fir trees were planted along the quay whilst coloured garlands, Chinese lanterns and flags decorated the Guildhall itself. A triumphal arch was raised outside the building bearing the inscriptions, 'Success to the Liskeard and Looe Railway; Welcome One and All.' The Directors of the Railway were also honoured with an address by the leading interests of the town. Progress and enterprise was linked directly with the railway.

On behalf of the inhabitants of Looe we cordially welcome you to our ancient town and we thank you for the great benefit you have conferred upon us by connecting Looe with the main railway system of the Kingdom.

We have no doubt that with the increased facilities you have now provided for visitors, this picturesque locality will bring more business and prosperity to the place and district, and we hope that the spirit of enterprise which you have shown will not go unrewarded and that you will share with us in the material advantages which will accrue from the advent of the railway.

A celebratory luncheon was provided in a marquee erected on the quay at East Looe, close to the Guildhall, with particular tributes, that day, going to Joseph Thomas for his efforts on behalf of the town. Together with his obvious achievements with regard to the railway, Joseph Thomas was also linked with other important local initiatives including construction of the Hannafore approach road to the town; the new building estate on the cliffs, encouraging the growth of Looe as a fashionable resort; with work in conjunction with the Harbour Commissioners to improve the pier and provide a powerful port light, and with the improvements in the water supply to the town. Three years earlier, in 1898, Looe had requested the assistance of the Local Government Board in the form of a sum of £2,500 to improve water supplies to West Looe. By way of lasting recognition, Joseph Thomas was also presented with a silver bowl for his services.

To conclude this brief account of the day's events it is useful to note that, excluding those who travelled on the Director's train, over 400 passengers visited Looe for the occasion. One particular party from Plymouth suffered something of an upset when at the end of the day their train failed to reach Liskeard in time for the last connecting service to Plymouth. They were rescued from their plight by the intervention of Mr Holbrook, the Company's Traffic Manager. In consultations with the Great Western staff he arranged for a special working to Plymouth, paid for by the Liskeard and Looe Company.

In keeping with its new progressive image the station at Looe was much improved. The lines to the quays controlled by the Harbour Commissioners obviously ran into the town itself, but the passenger station was a short distance north of the main community. Overlooking the river, the station was built on the east side of the line close to the roadway. It comprised a single platform with stone-built accommodation for a booking hall, booking office and station master's office, ladies waiting room and goods offices. Building work was carried out by Mr J. Taylor of Looe. Of the facilities described, the ladies waiting room was newly added, together with the lamp room and platform canopy, whilst the signalbox was enlarged and the platform lengthened by 125 feet to give overall length of 200 feet. The waiting room was decorated in similar style to that at Liskeard, and the station was lit by gas. An attractive lawn and garden area was laid out between the station and the river, and in later

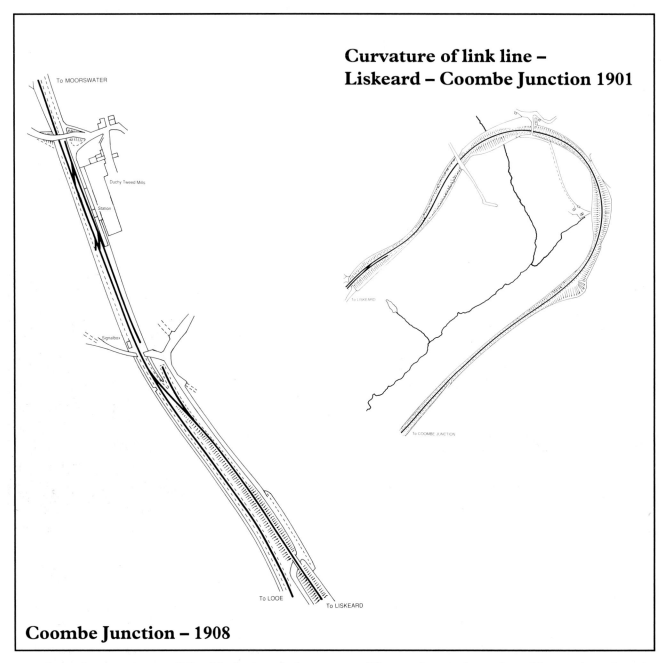

**Curvature of link line –
Liskeard – Coombe Junction 1901**

To MOORSWATER

Duchy Tweed Mills

Station

Signalbox

To LISKEARD

To COOMBE JUNCTION

To LOOE

To LISKEARD

Coombe Junction – 1908

years the station name was carefully picked out on the lawn in varieties of plants, adding to the appeal of the station generally. Proposals were also put forward during the celebrations of May 1901, for a 'Thames Embankment' style development from Looe Bridge to the station by way of further improvement.

To the south of the station was a small engine shed, and beyond this a carriage shed measuring 100 feet in length. Sidings and loops were easily accommodated on the wide river bank between the station and the town bridge, linking East and West Looe. A cattle market was later provided just to the north of the station, with direct access to the loading bank. This was a development dating from 1902, livestock proving to be a most useful source of revenue on the line.

Causeland and Sandplace, the intermediate stops, were described at the time as 'old buildings of the primitive type.' It was hoped to rebuild them. St Keyne opened October 1902.

The new locomotive and coaching stock used on the Directors special train aroused interest. Built by Robert Stephenson and Company Ltd of Newcastle, *Looe* was an 0-6-0 saddle tank. The coaching stock, described as similar to that on the New York Overhead Railway, was most unusual.

The latter comprised the composite first and second class vehicle with a guard's compartment, and two third class coaches, one also with a guard's compartment. They were said to be 'uniformly constructed on the American plan' with entrance via a platform area at each end. Theirs was an open design, not the compartment stock so well favoured in Britain. The overall length of these eight-wheeled bogie coaches was 40 feet including the end platform area, the latter having canopies to give shelter. Underframe construction was of pitch-pine, with an oak body; the floors and roof were of pitch-pine. First class furnishings included reversible blue cushions with

'4575' class No. 5534 leaves Coombe Junction with the 11.25 am Liskeard–Looe on 15th March 1960. Maximum speed allowed on the branch between Coombe Junction and Looe was 25 mph with many further restrictions en route. *P. Gray*

wax-cloth floor coverings and tapestry style curtains sliding on brass rods. Panelling was also provided to give the interior a more attractive finish. Pitch-pine was alternated with sequoia in order to achieve an effect where both light and darker woods complement one another. Brass lamps were provided for lighting. Second class accommodation offered horse-hair cushions whilst ceilings were painted white and were picked out with polished mahogany mouldings. Third class seating was of 'pitch-pine with fancy turned legs.' The stock was built by Hunt, Nelson and Co Ltd of Motherwell and was fitted with vacuum brakes.

One week after the official opening the locomotive *Looe* was derailed at Coombe Junction. Working the 8.35 pm service from Looe, the train stood at the station whilst the engine prepared to run round to complete the journey, in reverse direction, up to Liskeard. The driver ran the engine over the main line passing a ground disc signal at danger, and derailed the locomotive in the process. Whilst he escaped practically unhurt, the fireman suffered severe concussion from being thrown down. The 9.30 pm 'down' train from Liskeard was obviously delayed but on the following morning normal services were resumed, all running to time. The passengers on the derailed service of the Wednesday evening, however, suffered some delay as the replacement engine, being short of steam for the heavy ascent to Liskeard, had to make two trips, taking half the train at a time. Under the direction of the Engineer, Mr Thomas, rails were laid beneath the wheels of the locomotive and it was re-railed the next day.

Much better news for the period immediately after the opening was that in the first thirteen days of operation a total of 2,691 passengers had travelled over the line. 1,024 passengers booked tickets from Liskeard and intermediate stations whilst 1,037 booked from Looe and a further 630 from intermediate stops. Goods traffic was described as very satisfactory. Whitsun also brought large numbers of passengers with some 300 people leaving Liskeard on Whit-Monday in the first two trains of the day alone. Special services advertised for the day were as follows: From Liskeard, dep 9.45 am, 10.30; 1.10 pm; 2.20, 5.00, 7.40 and 9.45. From Looe, dep 8.30 am, 11.50, 3.45, 5.50, 6.20, 8.20, 9.20 pm. Excursion tickets were also issued at considerably reduced prices.

The value of the new link with the Great Western Railway was demonstrated in much increased traffic return over a period of time also. During 1902, passengers numbered over 55,000 and by the end of the decade the figures had more than trebled on their pre-1901 total.

In the midst of growth and opportunity, however, came a damaging set back. On 15th April 1906 the Liskeard and Looe suffered its worst accident, the result of a runaway from the Liskeard terminus.

51

No. 4565 leaves Coombe Junction and passes the signalbox with the 12.15 pm Looe–Liskeard service on 15th August 1959. The speed limit on the fierce winding climb to Liskeard was 15 mph, the same limit applying for the descent. *P. Gray*

The story really began the previous day, Thursday, when the Company ran a 12 coach special working from Looe to Liskeard and on to Doublebois forming an outing by the Looe Wesleyan Sunday School. Six of these coaches were worked back from Looe to Liskeard the following day at the rear of a goods train to Moorswater. At the latter place they were detached and then taken up to Liskeard by the locomotive *Kilmar*. The train arrived at the upper terminus soon after 6 pm without any problems, but whilst uncoupling the locomotive from the train, the driver was asked to set the engine back slightly in order to ease the coupling. In doing so the locomotive also gave the coaches something of a push causing them to run backwards. It was reported that it had been a very wet day, following a reasonably dry spell, this making the rails greasy. The coaches ran backward down the gradient, despite the efforts of railway men to stop them by putting stones on the line. Prompt action by the Liskeard and Looe signalman, however, in telephoning Coombe Junction box, enabled the signalman there to hold the oncoming 6 pm passenger from Looe at the distant signal. In the meantime, the errant stock gathered speed to what was said at the time to be 60 to 70 miles per hour, and miraculously stayed on the line to pass through Coombe Junction bound for Moorswater, with staff for the most part helpless onlookers.

At Moorswater there were up to six lines that the runaway might take. In fact, the points were set for the carriage works and it was here that the real damage was done. Two coaches were standing outside the shed, and the first was telescoped by the impact. They failed to stop the runaway, however, and the entire mass burst through the shed doors, 'parting them like paper.' A contemporary report gave a vivid description of the scene at that stage –

> Cannoning into the carriages inside the shed, the latter were driven clean through the end wall of brick, and forced into the meadow beyond, keeping upright, however. At the same moment the whole of the side of the shed on the near side collapsed, together with a considerable part of the iron roof. – The two carriages which met in the shock were piled up one over the other, being battered out of all semblence of their former shape, the sides and flooring being reduced to matchwood.

The three Hurst-Nelson coaches were almost completely destroyed by the impact, but five of the six runaway coaches were intact. Scarcely a window was broken in them it was claimed, but damage was done to the frames, buffer springs and drawbars. Emergency stock was bought in from the Mersey Railway, and, after 1909, when the GWR ran the line, the latter company introduced its own stock. The Great Western also hired out one of its locomotives to the line, a 4-4-0 saddle tank, No. 13, which continued to work the branch for many years.

With final reference to the accident, it was indeed fortunate that there was no loss of life. Carpenters had been working until 5 pm on raising the roof of the locomotive shed whilst painters had earlier been at work on one of the coaches in the shed. Had they been on the site at the time of the impact, they would most surely have been injured at the very least.

One further accident, giving an opportunity to mention freight traffic, can be considered here. On 28th March 1908 a goods train from Looe caught fire at Landlooe Bridge, between Causeland and St Keyne. The incident took place at 12.30 pm and involved two wagons of hay and one of straw. They were covered by tarpaulins and when the driver looked back along his train he saw that the tarpaulins on one of the straw wagons was burning. Sparks from the locomotive had caused the fire. The train was stopped but by this time two wagons were alight. These were uncoupled and the locomotive *Cheesewring* and the remainder of the train, which included a consignment of cattle, went on to Coombe Junction. The locomotive returned carrying as many men as possible to help fight the fire. With the help of the local people of Landlooe the blaze was brought under control and extinguished. During the proceedings it was necessary to pour large amounts of water on the timber sleepers so as to avoid them catching fire. With the fire out and the wagons saved, the trains moved on to Coombe allowing the delayed 1.15 pm service for Liskeard to pass. The straw and hay was part of a consignment of some 4 to 5 tons bound for a forage dealer at Plymouth.

China clay traffic also became part of the scene from 1904 when the St Neots Clay Company built their clay dry at Moorswater. A pipeline fed the dry with clay from Parsons Park pit near St Neot. Agreement was reached for the pipeline in February 1902 when the 'seal of the Council' was granted, giving the St Neots Company permission to run their pipes across the highway at various points on the route from Parson Park to Moorswater. The first consignment of clay to Looe was moved in November 1904, increasing activity at the port. Goods and mineral traffic comprising agricultural supplies, livestock, general merchandise, together with coal, granite, sand and the china clay, ensured that freight services on the line were kept busy.

Whilst this encouraging situation happily applied to the Liskeard and Looe sections, circumstances were much less hopeful on the Caradon line. Deprived of the once rich copper ore traffic from the mines the line north of Moorswater had little to offer financially. Hopes were raised when a new company was formed in 1908 to rework the Phoenix United sett. With capital of £100,000 the new Prince of Wales shaft was sunk, with an imposing new engine house forming part of the surface workings. Large scale drainage and exploration got underway with the assistance of modern machinery, but six years later, with little in the way of positive returns the mine was forced to close. Further investment was called for but in the economic climate of 1914 and the urgent financial demands made by the First World War, money was not to be found. Development at Phoenix United ceased from August 1914.

With the closure of this last venture, mining ceased on Caradon Hill bringing to an end what had been a spectacular period of prosperity and change for the district. Closure took place for the entire railway system north of Moorswater from 1st January 1917, the rails being lifted and put to more effective use elsewhere. Since 1909 the Caradon line had been the property of the GWR who also worked the Liskeard and Looe Railway from that time. This had come about via the Great Western, Liskeard and Looe and Liskeard and Caradon Railway Act of 25th May 1909. Under the Railways Act of 1921, of course, the Liskeard and Looe also became part of the GWR.

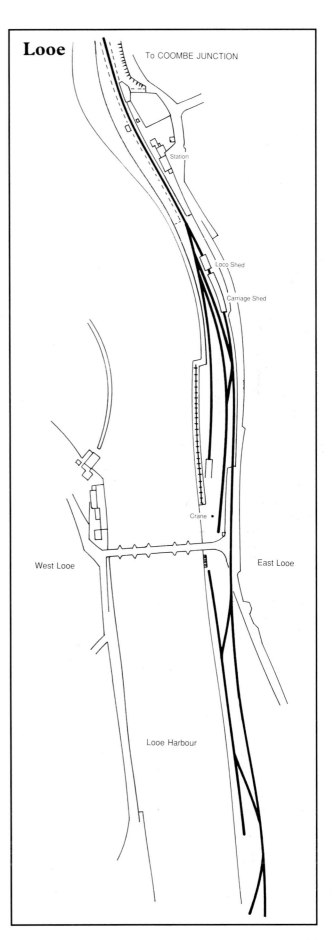

Looe

To COOMBE JUNCTION

Station

Loco Shed

Carriage Shed

Crane

West Looe

East Looe

Looe Harbour

Chapter Eight

Liskeard – Looe: GWR

The GWR played a decisive part in the development of Looe between the two world wars. It was as a resort that the town made its best progress, but it continued also to be a working port. With easy access via the railway, the population of the Looe Urban District increased considerably. From June 1922 to June 1932, for example, the area showed a 6.2 per cent increase whilst from 1931 to 1939 the increase was 7.2. This was in direct contrast with several other inland areas, as, for example, the Liskeard Rural District which declined by 7.2 per cent, and the Municipal Borough which declined by 3 per cent. From 1939 to 1948 the Looe Urban District population increased by 22.9, second only in improvement to Newquay at 32.7 per cent.

Perhaps the best indication of the growth of the town and district as a popular holiday area was the decision on the part of the GWR to build a new single line branch from Trerulefoot, on the main line west of St Germans to Looe itself. Authorised under the Great Western Railway (Additional Powers) Act of 1936 the new route was intended to provide passengers with a journey of only 35 minutes, to and from Plymouth ending the need to change trains at Liskeard, and the time consuming business of reversal at Coombe Junction. As planned, the new route would be heavily engineered, requiring no less than three tunnels and two substantial viaducts. A new station was also needed, this being on the high ground to the south-east of the existing station. The Urban Council was strongly opposed to this

A view at the turn of the century looking inland showing the two communities of East and West Looe. The station at East Looe can be seen beyond the bridge, likewise the rail links down onto the quays themselves. Vast tonnages of copper ore and granite had travelled to the quayside here with coal for the mines and fish for various markets being taken up by the railway. The photograph also shows how closely the track followed the riverline winding its way inland towards Sandplace. Tourism is the mainspring of the local economy today.
Cornwall Local Studies Library

Liskeard branch platform as seen in the early 1920s. Opened in May 1901, this link line curving across and down the Liskeard Valley on its opposite side made the final connection with Looe. Set at right-angles to the main line, the branch platform was extended in 1924 and again in 1937.

Cornwall Local Studies Library

Looking along the Looe branch platform at Liskeard. This view of 29th September 1959 shows '4575' class 2-6-2T No. 4585 in the process of running round its train. The platform here was at right angles to the main line behind the photographer. Opened officially on 15th May 1901, passenger trains, in fact, began on 8th May that year. The branch platform was twice extended after this date, first in 1924 and again in 1937 giving an overall length of 640 feet.

P. Gray

The line curves away into the first of a succession of deep cuttings and embankments on its down-hill run to Coombe Junction. The speed limit between Liskeard and Coombe Junction was 15 mph in GWR days. 10th July 1955.   *R.C. Riley*

chosen site given the difficult access and the climb from the town itself. Stations were also planned for Hessenford, Seaton and Millendreath.

In June 1936 it was reported that four miles of foreshore between Millendreath and Downderry had been purchased from the Duchy of Cornwall. Trial borings on the tunnel sites had also taken place, whilst rumours connected with this particular work suggested that proposals were afoot to build giant oil storage tanks beneath the hills at Seaton to protect these vital supplies from possible enemy attack.

The GWR hotel planned as an essential feature of the new scheme was to occupy a dramatic 20 acre clifftop location offering every attraction. Tennis and squash courts, a bowling green, putting and a bathing pool were to form part of the site which also included the possibility of an escalator to give guests easy access to and from the private bathing beach. A new golf course was also under construction. The long term objective of the railway company, was made quite clear. In their own words, it was stated:

The desire of the GWR was to help the development of Looe by the establishment of a high class residential neighbourhood.

When asked about public access along the foreshore the official response from the Company was equally clear:

We are going to spend a sum in the neighbourhood of £100,000 to £150,000 and we don't want every Tom, Dick or Harry wandering about.

It was also said, however, that there was no objection to the public walking along the foreshore.

Despite the formidable engineering works required to build the line it was hoped that services would commence in 1939 or 1940. This, of course, was not to be. Work was underway by the latter part of 1937, but the line was never to get beyond the preliminary stages of construction before the scheme was abandoned. The onset of World War Two would have brought development to a halt, whilst the climate of austerity in the post-war world ruled out any such initiatives.

Had it been completed the new line would have given the branch a decisive new orientation towards Plymouth and the east, being ideal for tourist traffic from other parts of Britain. It would also certainly have brought changes, and likely closure, for the old line via Coombe Junction, which was difficult and expensive to work with its gradients, curvature and reversal procedures.

On the branch itself there were several pointers to increased business between the wars. At Looe and Liskeard the platforms were lengthened to contend with increased traffic. In 1928 the platform at Looe was extended southward towards the town by 96 feet, whilst at Liskeard the branch platform was twice extended, in 1924 and 1937, giving an overall length of 640 feet. The goods yard at Liskeard was also enlarged.

The timetable on the branch in October 1909, the first year that it was worked by the GWR, was as follows:

Having just passed beneath Liskeard viaduct, '4500' class 2-6-2T No. 4565 brings the 8.40 am 'Looe Express' up the eastern slope of the Liskeard Valley on the fierce 1 in 40 gradient. On slightly easier gradients above this section the train will cross the valley to the western slope turning eventually some 270 degrees. *P. Gray*

In delightfully rural surroundings '4500' class No. 4569 leaves Causeland with the 2.52 pm Liskeard–Looe, on 19th April 1960. Causeland was the only intermediate station between Moorswater and Looe when passenger services began on 11th September 1879. *P. Gray*

A Great Western scene of the 1920s as seen from the carriage window. A '4500' class 2-6-2T between Sandplace and Causeland is working up the valley with a train from Looe. The branch fulfilled all expectations for those in search of the definitive GWR rural railway, offering a wide variety of landscape and operating practice.
Cornwall Local Studies Library Redruth

Timetable October 1909

				Sat					Sun	
Liskeard	5.30	9.12	10.55	1.15	2.40	4.55	7.30	9.40	5.30	8.15
Coombe Jct.	5.40	9.22	11.05	1.25	2.50	5.05	7.40	9.50	5.40	8.25
St Keyne	5.45	9.27	11.10	1.30	2.55	5.10	7.45	9.55	5.45	8.30
Causeland	-	9.31	11.14	1.34	2.59	5.14	7.49	9.59	-	8.34
Sandplace	5.54	9.36	11.19	1.39	3.04	5.19	7.54	10.04	5.54	8.39
Looe	6.00	9.42	11.25	1.45	3.10	5.25	8.00	10.10	6.00	8.45

	Mons				Sat			Sun	
Looe	6.45	8.25	10.00	12.15	2.00	3.55	6.40	8.30	6.50
Sandplace	6.51	8.31	10.06	12.21	2.06	4.01	6.46	8.36	6.56
Causeland	6.56	8.36	10.11	12.26	2.11	4.06	6.51	8.41	7.01
St Keyne	7.00	8.40	10.15	12.30	2.15	4.10	6.55	8.45	7.05
Coombe Jct.	7.07	8.47	10.22	12.37	2.22	4.17	7.02	8.52	7.12
Liskeard	7.15	8.55	10.30	12.45	2.30	4.25	7.10	9.00	7.20

This compared well with the service of the early 1930s for example. In the summer timetable of 1932 there were ten trains to Looe, including the last two of the day, 9.05 and 10.30 pm, Saturdays only. The earliest departed at 7.25 am with the final train at 7.35 pm Mon-Fri. No Sunday service was provided although this was reintroduced the following year. Journey times in 1932 showed an improvement generally of one to two minutes.

Special seasonal workings can be appreciated by examining one particular year, 1936, when Britain was over the worst of the depression afflicting the early thirties. Easter Monday, April 13th, brought increased traffic. Cheap day trips from Liskeard to Looe were offered at 1 shilling and 3 pence (6p) with departures at 9.00 am, 9.55, 11.20, 1.30 pm and 3.05. Whitsun also brought large numbers of people, whilst on August Bank Holiday Regatta Day, it was estimated that some 10,000 people visited Looe. Heavy Bank Holiday traffic, particularly when the day coincided with a special event such as a regatta, had long been established. In the later Edwardian years regatta days at Looe could see a special service of up to 12 trains in each direction.

Looe had plenty to offer the visitor. *The Homeland Handbook* of 1913 included a vivid description of the town, capturing its special character and strong sense of history. With reference to the old town of East Looe it was said:

It would be futile to try to outline a route through this neighbourhood. It is a delight for the visitor to plunge into the network and come out where he can. It is a congeries of streets, courts, alleys and opening, mostly cobbled and pebbled occupying a level spit of land. There are old houses and cottages, with projecting stories, outside stairways or heavy buttresses, gabled, recessed edged and corbelled out, with corners sliced off

Above: A spectacular panoramic view showing the 4.35 pm Liskeard–Looe service running down the valley between Causeland and Sandplace. The rural character of the line is once again well illustrated here.   *P. Gray*

Right: Sandplace again, this time on 15th August 1959. '4500' class No. 4565 leaves with the 1.23 Liskeard–Looe. A GWR cast iron notice can be seen on the side of the hut; a bench, oil lamp and the open platform complete the scene. Note the signpost helping to add interest to this quiet attractive location.   *P. Gray*

or undercut for passage, with stone-mullioned windows, pointed and Tudor doorways, pent houses and dormers, passages, courtyards and cellars - such an odd irregular collection - no two houses with the same front or general appearance - as you will get hardly anywhere else in Cornwall.

Looe Guide 1936

		s.	d.
(1)	Rail and Sea – Plymouth. On Wednesdays and Saturdays: Out by train, Looe to Plymouth Home by Steamer, Plymouth to Looe	3	6
(2)	Road and Rail – Fowey. On Weekdays: Out by Bus via Polperro to Polruan, Home, Fowey to Looe by train, via the Glynn Valley; scenery deserving of special mention	3	6
(3)	Fal River Tour (Truro and Falmouth). On certain weekdays: According to the tides. Full particulars gladly supplied at the GWR Station	7	6
(4)	St Keyne's Well. Rail to St Keyne, walk to the well and return by rail from Causeland	0	8
(5)	St Cuby's Well and Stone Circle, Duloe. Rail to Sandplace, turn left over bridge and up the hill to Duloe	0	4
(6)	Eddystone Lighthouse. See local advertisements: By GWR fully-licensed steamer	1	6

This was of course, ideal for GWR publicity purposes but Looe was careful to offer an effective blend of the traditional and the modern to appeal to all its visitors. Mindful of the past, the resort also looked to the future.

A new golf links at Ben Downs was opened in May 1936 with putting and bowling greens in 1937. The beaches and cliffs would always beckon lovers of the outdoors, as indeed, did the many boat trips available from the resort. During the season of 1936, GWR steamers brought over 10,000 people to Looe, from Plymouth. Many also enjoyed the advertised trips around the Eddystone Lighthouse. The following year saw an increase, to just over 16,000 people visiting the resort by sea. A round trip between Plymouth and Looe combining rail and steamer services offered an interesting opportunity to enjoy a wide variety of sea and landscapes. The return fare, as advertised for 1936, was 3/6d, being available on Wednesdays and Saturdays. For less sunny days there was also the alternative of the Cinema; Looe having its 'Pavillion' and 'Merry Little Cinema' to cater for film goers. The attraction and popularity of the Cinema should not be ignored at this particular period in time. Returning outdoors, the district had a great deal to offer away from the coast. The beautifully wooded East Looe river valley and the magnificent estuary offered a gentler, more contemplative landscape, in contrast with the vigour and bustle of the coast. The Holidays with Pay Act of 1938 was especially important for the tourist industry allowing greater opportunities for families throughout Britain to enjoy at least one week 'beside the seaside'. Looe, like all other resorts, could only benefit.

Special cheap fares on long-distance trains serving important national events also underlined the fact that Looe was not a remote and isolated location. Taking events of 1936, special fares were offered on the 8.15 pm from Looe to meet an overnight service eastward at Liskeard. Amongst specific trains for London at a fare of 19 shillings, were other specials covering the Grand National, with a service to Birkenhead, 27th March at £1.00; the FA Cup at Wembley, Arsenal – Sheffield United, 24th April; The Derby, 27th May, and the International Horse Show at Olympia, 5th June.

Clay traffic to the port, controlled on the dock itself by the Harbour Commissioners, was one example of freight traffic on the branch. Coal for domestic purposes for the gasworks at Looe and for the clay dry at Moorswater was also valuable, whilst agriculture and the livestock trade was particularly enhanced by the railway.

The potato trade had long been of value. In 1846, before the arrival of the railway, the 'Report on the Farming of Cornwall' included the following:

'In parishes bordering on Looe great quantities of potatoes are grown for the London market. In some parishes which adjoin the cliffs and the river where seaweed can be obtained at small expense, the greater portion of the land intended for wheat is first planted to potatoes.'

In 1902 the Urban Council considered the development of the cattle trade. Whilst a date of February 1902 takes the story back beyond the working control of the GWR developments pursued at that time reflected the climate of opportunity and change, which later worked to the advantage of the GWR. The following statement was made to the Council for their consideration:

With the advent of improved railway communications quite a brisk trade in cattle, amongst other commodities, has sprung up in the Looe district, and a feeling has been growing amongst farmers and dealers of the neighbouring parishes that it would be a good thing to establish a monthly cattle market at Looe. At present the nearest fair is one held at Liskeard on the second Monday of each month, but that town is deemed by some to be too far distant to convey livestock, while it is held that an important district around Polperro extending to Lanteglos and northward to Pelynt, Lanreath and even Duloe would be glad to make Looe a centre. –

The Chairman of the Liskeard and Looe Railway Company pledged to afford every facility for a market making it clear that it was very much the work of the Company to develop trade in the district. A further offer of land for the market was made to the Urban Council, the site being that adjoining the station immediately to the north.

Whilst the development of such trade was welcomed by many, there were those with reservations. It was pointed out that growth in the livestock trade might well clash with the town's image as a resort. This conflict between the interests of traditional trade and the growing demands of tourism was a factor that brought about considerable debate in Cornish coastal towns. In every case it was a difficult question to resolve. Whereas at Penzance there were complaints at fish traffic moving through the streets, to the detriment of a fashionable image, so at Looe a critic voiced fears about the livestock market

The town is looked upon as a residential seaside resort and cattle being driven through the streets would not be a pleasing sight to the residents or visitors.

Below Sandplace the valley broadens out and the river enjoys a wide expanse with tidal waters adding to the character of the line. The railway runs along the riverside on a low embankment allowing for spectacular views of the water and wildlife. '4575' class No. 4585 is seen here at Terras Crossing on 11th July 1959 working down to Looe. The close proximity of the river and the railway embankment are clearly illustrated here.   *P. Gray*

Springtime in the Looe Valley. '4500' class No. 4569 runs alongside the tidal waters near Terras Crossing as it works the 11.55 am Liskeard–Looe on 19th April 1960.   *P. Gray*

Railway staff pose in front of the *Lady Margaret* as it stands with two freight wagons at Looe early this century. Note the timetables and posters displayed on the station. *Lady Margaret*, a 2-4-0T, worked the branch from 1902 until shortly after World War One and survived elsewhere until 1948.

Cornwall Local Studies Library

Looe was also, of course, a fishing port. In many respects this added to its appeal for tourists looking to appreciate the atmosphere of the traditional fishing community. GWR poster work between the wars certainly portrayed Looe as a characteristic Cornish fishing port, taking care also to include views of the beaches, to give the broadest appeal.

Under official classification Looe was considered one of Cornwall's five major ports; Newlyn, Mevagissey, St Ives and Padstow being the others. Looe, Mevagissey and Padstow, however, were never as large as Newlyn or St Ives, all three ports accounting for only 12 to 14 per cent collectively of the total catch from 1919-1938. Despite this, Looe has enjoyed good trade in crabs, lobsters and crawfish, being, with St Ives, a leader in this aspect of the industry. With its ability to offer swift movement the railway made it possible to transport fresh fish to other parts of Britain with little problem. The fishery at Looe included catches of herring, mackerel and pilchards.

Returning to passenger traffic it is useful to compare and contrast the timetable of the post-war years. Nationalisation itself brought little outward change, whilst the impact of the Holidays with Pay Act, combined with the eventual ending of austerity, made the final years of steam working a busy period. The summer timetable for 1959, for instance, gave a service of nine trains to Looe, Mondays to Fridays, with ten on Saturdays. There were also nine workings from Looe to Liskeard, Mondays to Fridays, with twelve trains on Saturdays. A Sunday service of six trains in each direction completed the timetable. This service, overall, indicated a high standard of performance on the branch comparing most favourably with what had gone before and with that which was to follow. Ten years later, the summer timetable of 1969 still offered a pattern of nine trains each way, Mondays to Fridays, with ten trains operating on Summer Saturdays. A Sunday service gave six trains in each direction.

The 1960s, however, had brought considerable change.

In November 1963 freight services south of Coombe Junction were withdrawn. The harbour lines at Looe had been removed considerably earlier, in 1954. Detailed alterations to the trackwork accompanied the closure to goods, with sidings being taken out of use in November 1963 and lifted the following year. April 28th 1968 marked a further rationalisation when the platform was shortened at the south end. Today, there is no pointwork at Looe, only the branch line itself serving the town with usually no more than a single car DMU.

At the time of writing, December 1988, there are nine trains in each direction, Mondays to Saturdays. There is no Sunday service. A day return ticket, obtained from the guard, is priced at £1.87. Stopping at all stations, the journey time is 30 minutes. Clay trains, thankfully, still operate from Moorswater to Liskeard. The signalbox at Coombe Junction was closed in 1981 and replaced by a ground frame, operated by the guard. A second ground frame beyond Coombe Junction station controls movement to and from the clay dry at Moorswater.

The most conspicuous change on the branch in the early 1960s was the demise of steam locomotives and their replacement with more modern forms of traction. Steam working ceased on 11th September 1961 just over a century after its introduction. Following nationalisation the motive power on the line remained the '4500/4575' class 2-6-2 T, working passenger and freight turns alike. These locomotives had been busy on the line in the years before the outbreak of World War Two. The smaller '4400' 2-6-2 T were also used, and any one of these distinctively Great Western locomotives, so well known to the Company's West Country branch lines, must have made a magnificent sight running up and down the wonderful Looe Valley.

The sights and sounds of the branch in steam days belong now to the past. Even so, one can still appreciate something of the character and spirit of the line through the mind's eye. Take a fine summer's morning in the immediate pre-war years, perhaps. With the river closeby, sparkling and dancing its way to the sea; with the sharp clarity of a whistle, ringing through the trees and echoing across the valley; and, with the sight and sound of the train itself in sunlight, shadow and steam, it was clear that the railway, most surely, belonged to that landscape, no less than the streams and lanes that had defined it for centuries.

Table 96 **LISKEARD and LOOE**

Miles		Week Days																Sundays					
		am S	am	am S	am E	am E	am S	am S	noon E	pm	pm N	pm E	pm S	pm N	pm E	pm S	pm S	am	am	pm	pm	pm	pm
—	Liskeard .. .. .. dep	545	7 15	8 45	8 55	9 52	10 5	1125	12 0	1 23	2 52	4 35	4 40	5 50	720	7 45	9 13	9 0	1035	12 15	2 10	4 35	7 40
2	Coombe Junction Halt ..	...	7 23	8 55	9 3	10 5	1015	1133	12 8	1 33	3 3	4 45	4 50	5 59	730	7 54	9 22	9 8	1043	12 23	2 18	4 43	7 48
3¾	St. Keyne Halt	.	7 28	9 0	9 8	1010	1021	1138	1213	1 36	3 8	4 50	4 55	6 4	735	7 58	9 26	9 13	1048	12 28	2 23	4 48	7 53
5	Causeland Halt	...	7 32	9 5	9 12	1014	1026	1142	1217	1 40	3 12	4 54	4 59	6 8	739	8 2	9 30	9 17	1052	12 32	2 27	4 52	7 57
6½	Sandplace Halt	.	7 37	9 9	9 17	1018	1030	1146	1222	1 45	3 16	4 58	5 3	6 12	743	8 7	9 35	9 22	1057	12 37	2 31	4 57	8 2
8¾	Looe .... arr	620	7 44	9 17	9 24	1025	1037	1155	1230	1 53	3 23	5 5	5 10	6 20	750	8 14	9 42	9 30	11 5	12 45	2 40	5 5	8 10

Miles		Week Days																	Sundays					
		am S	am S	am E	am S	am S	am E	am S	am E	pm S	pm E	pm	pm	pm N	pm E	pm S	pm	pm S	am	am	pm	pm	pm	pm
—	Looe .. .. dep	635	7 50	8 10	840	9 30	9 42	1045	1050	1215	1240	2 0	345	5 10	6 27	640	830	9 50	9 45	11 20	1 25	2 50	6 30	8 20
2¼	Sandplace Halt	...	7 56	8 16	...	9 35	9 48	1050	1055	1221	1246	2 6	351	5 16	6 32	645	836	9 55	9 51	11 26	1 30	2 56	6 36	8 26
3¾	Causeland Halt	.	8 0	8 20	.	9 39	9 52	1054	11 0	1225	1250	210	355	5 20	6 36	649	840	9 59	9 55	11 30	1 34	3 0	6 40	8 30
5	St. Keyne Halt	...	8 4	8 24	...	9 43	9 56	1058	11 4	1229	1254	214	4 0	5 24	6 40	653	844	10 3	9 59	11 34	1 38	3 4	6 44	8 34
6¾	Coombe Junction Halt ..	.	8 14	8 32	.	9 53	10 5	11 6	1111	1236	1 1	222	410	5 33	6 48	7 1	851	1010	10 7	11 42	1 47	3 12	6 52	8 42
8¾	Liskeard .... arr	7 5	8 24	8 42	910	10 2	1015	1117	1122	1246	1 11	233	420	5 45	6 58	711	9 1	1021	1016	11 52	1 58	3 22	7 1	8 51

E Except Saturdays **N** 5 minutes later on Saturdays **S** Saturdays only

Table 97 **BODMIN ROAD, BODMIN GENERAL, WADEBRIDGE and PADSTOW**

WEEK DAYS ONLY (Z)

Miles from Bodmin Road	Miles from Bodmin Nth		am S	am B	am	am T	am	am	am E	am E	am S	am S	am G	am N		am S	am	pm E	noon S	pm S	pm E	pm S	pm E
—		Bodmin Road .. .. dep	6 55	.	..	7 50	..	..	.	9 0	915	..	10 5	10 10	..	1040	..	..	12 0	..	1220	1238	1 5
3½		Bodmin Gen A.. arr	7 10	...	...	7 58	...	...	...	910	923	...	1013	10 18	...	1048	...	...	1210	...	1228	1248	1 13
		Bodmin Gen A.. dep	..	.	7 30	8 10	..	..	9 0	.	.	..	1020	10 35	..	..	..	..	..	..	1236	1251	..
—	—	Bodmin North. dep	...	...	...	...	8 43	...	...	...	...	...	...	...	...	...	11 20	...	...	...	...	...	...
—	1½	Dunmere Halt	..	.	..	..	8 47	..	.	.	.	..	..	..	..	..	11 24	..	..	..	..	..	..
6½	2¼	Nanstallon Halt	...	...	7 37	8 18	8 50	...	...	...	...	...	...	...	...	...	11 27	...	...	...	1245	1258	...
8	3¾	Grogley Halt	..	.	7 42	..	8 54	..	.	.	.	..	..	..	..	..	11 31	..	..	..	..	..	..
11	6¾	Wadebridge.. arr	...	...	7 51	8 30	9 2	...	918	...	...	...	1037	10 52	...	...	11 39	...	...	...	1257	1 10	...
		Wadebridge.. dep	..	716	7 53	8 40	..	9K17	.	.	.	1015	1040	11 15	..	..	11K40	12 3	..	1220	..	..	..
16½	12¾	Padstow .... arr	...	726	8 3	8 50	...	9K27	...	...	...	1024	1049	11 24	...	...	11K50	1214	...	1230	...	...	...

	pm S	pm	pm C	pm	pm	pm S	pm S	pm E	pm S	pm E	pm E	pm E	pm S	pm S	pm E	pm	pm T	pm	pm	pm S	pm T	pm	pm S
Bodmin Road .. .. dep	1 22	..	..	..	2 30	3 20	..	..	..	..	4 25	..	4 55	..	..	..	6 15	..	7 26	8 0	9 5	9 42	1050
Bodmin Gen. A.. arr	1 30	...	...	...	2 38	3 35	...	...	...	...	4 33	...	5 5	...	...	...	6 25	...	7 35	8 8	9 16	9 50	1058
Bodmin Gen. A.. dep	..	..	..	..	2 48	..	..	..	..	..	4 50	.	5 18	..	..	..	6 35	..	7 43	..	9 20	..	..
Bodmin North. dep	...	...	...	2 0	...	...	4 5	4 23	...	...	...	...	...	5 36	5 44	...	...	...	...	...	...	...	...
Dunmere Halt	..	..	..	2 4	..	..	4 9	4 27	..	..	..	..	..	5 40	5 48	..	..	..	..	..	..	..	..
Nanstallon Halt	...	...	...	2 7	...	...	4 12	4 30	...	...	4 57	...	5 27	5 43	5 51	...	6 42	...	7 50	...	9 29	...	...
Grogley Halt	..	..	..	2 11	..	..	4 16	4 34	..	..	..	..	..	5 47	5 55	..	6 47	..	..	..	9 33	..	..
Wadebridge .. arr	...	...	...	2 19	3 6	...	4 24	4 42	...	...	5 9	...	5 39	5 55	6 3	...	6 55	...	8 2	...	9 41	...	...
Wadebridge .. dep	..	1 15	2 3	2 23	..	..	4 25	..	4 50	4 53	5 10	5 33	..	..	..	6 13	6 58	7 48	..	..	9 42	..	..
Padstow .... arr	...	1 29	2 14	2 34	...	...	4 35	...	5 0	5 3	5 19	5 42	...	...	...	6 22	7 9	7 58	...	...	9 52	...	...

Miles	Miles		am	am	am E	am	am S	am N	am E	am	am E	am T	am E	am		am G	am S	am S	am N	pm E	am E	pm S	pm E
—	—	Padstow .. .. dep	..	..	..	..	..	8 10	8 12	8 30	..	9K 3	9 33	..	..	1055	11 0	..	1135	..	1155	1210	1258
5½	5½	Wadebridge.. arr	...	...	...	...	...	8 19	8 21	8 39	...	9K12	9 42	...	...	11 4	11 9	...	1144	...	12 4	1219	1 7
		Wadebridge.. dep	6 58	..	..	8 1	..	8 30	8 30	..	..	9 19	..	9†48	..	11 7	..	..	1152	..	1225	1226	..
8½	8½	Grogley Halt	7 6	...	...	8 9	...	8 40	8 40	...	...	...	...	9†56	...	...	...	...	...	...	1233	1236	...
10	10	Nanstallon Halt . ..	7 10	..	..	8 13	..	8 44	8 44	..	..	9 32	..	10†0	..	1119	..	..	12 6	..	1237	1240	..
—	10¾	Dunmere Halt	...	...	...	8 17	...	...	...	...	...	...	...	10†4	...	...	...	...	...	...	1241	1244	...
—	12½	Bodmin North. arr	..	..	..	8 21	..	..	..	..	..	..	..	10†8	..	..	..	..	..	..	1245	1248	..
13	—	Bodmin Gen. A .. arr	7 20	...	...	...	...	8 55	8 55	...	...	9 42	...	...	...	1129	...	...	1215	...	...	...	...
		Bodmin Gen. A .. dep	..	7 25	8 15	..	8 30	8 58	..	..	9 18	9 45	..	..	..	1134	..	1134	1223	1245	..	..	..
16½	—	Bodmin Road.. .. arr	...	7 35	8 22	...	8 37	9 5	...	...	9 25	9 54	...	...	...	1141	...	1141	1230	1252	...	...	...

	pm S	pm S	pm	pm	pm	pm	pm S	pm		pm E	pm S		pm	pm	pm S	pm S	pm	pm	pm	pm		pm	pm S
Padstow .. .. dep	..	1 0	..	2 52	3 13	..	4 40	..	..	5 24	..	..	6 0	..	..	..	8 4	..	8 30	..	..	10 5	..
Wadebridge.. arr	...	1 9	...	3 1	3 22	...	4 49	...	...	5 33	...	...	6 9	...	...	...	8 13	...	8 39	...	...	1014	...
Wadebridge.. dep	..	..	1 23	3 7	..	3 24	..	5 11	..	5 34	..	..	..	6 12	7 0	..	..	8 17	..	8 42	..	..	..
Grogley Halt	...	...	1 31	3 17	...	...	...	5 19	...	...	...	...	...	6 20	...	...	...	8 25	...	...	...	...	...
Nanstallon Halt . ..	..	..	1 35	3 21	..	..	..	5 23	..	5 46	..	..	..	6 24	7 12	..	..	8 29	..	8 54	..	..	..
Dunmere Halt	...	...	...	3 25	...	...	...	5 27	...	...	...	...	...	...	...	...	...	...	...	...	...	...	...
Bodmin North. arr	..	..	..	3 29	..	..	..	5 31	..	..	..	..	..	..	..	..	..	..	..	..	..	..	..
Bodmin Gen. A .. arr	...	...	1 45	...	...	3 45	...	...	...	5 56	...	...	...	6 33	7 21	...	...	8 40	...	9 4	...	...	...
Bodmin Gen. A .. dep	1 0	..	1 50	..	..	3 53	..	..	..	6 0	6 0	..	..	6 43	..	7 38	..	8 44	..	9 15	..	..	1020
Bodmin Road.. .. arr	1 7	...	2 0	...	...	4 1	...	...	...	6 8	6 8	...	...	6 50	...	7 45	...	8 51	...	9 33	...	...	1027

A 1 mile to Bodmin North Station
B Saturdays only. Runs 15th July to 2nd September inclusive
C Saturdays only. Runs 1st July to 19th August inclusive
E Except Saturdays
G Except Saturdays. Through Trains between Bodmin Road and Padstow
K 5 minutes later on Saturdays
N Saturdays only. Through Train between Padstow and Bodmin Road
S Saturdays only
T Through Train between Bodmin Road and Padstow
Z On Sundays passengers holding through rail tickets may travel by Southern National Omnibus between Bodmin Road and Wadebridge or vice-versa—see Table 21
† 2 minutes later on Saturdays

Chapter Nine

Accidents on the Main Line

The main line east of Lostwithiel has seen several serious accidents, involving collisions, derailments and runaways. Most of them happened during the earlier years of the line, with three of the worst disasters, those of May 1859, December 1873 and April 1895, being covered here.

One of the most serious accidents was also the first visited upon the Cornwall Company. It took place at Grove Viaduct, between Saltash and St Germans, on the evening of Friday 6th May 1859, just two days after the line had opened.

The train involved was the 7.25 pm from Plymouth to Truro, comprising the locomotive *Elk*, two second class coaches, a first class vehicle set between the second class stock, and a goods wagon coupled to the rear. Most of the passengers had left the train at either Devonport or Saltash,

but as it continued westward, on the approach to Grove Viaduct, a sudden violent jerk was felt and the train left the rails.

From the immediate application of the brake by the rear guard, Richard Paddon, sufficient strain was put on the couplings to separate the locomotive and the first two coaches from the rear section of the train. This quick reaction saved those travelling in the third coach as it eventually came to rest a matter of yards onto the viaduct with the leading wheels derailed. The locomotive and front coaches, however, having damaged the track for almost 150 years, ran out onto the viaduct and finally plunged through the parapet and down into the creek, 38 feet below. The locomotive lay parallel with the viaduct, but had turned over completely with its wheels in the air and the boiler chimney and cab being buried several feet in the mud. Both coaches

The scene at the accident in the Fowey Valley on Saturday 16th April 1895. Following damage to the 'down' line by the previous train, 'The Cornishman', apparently running at excessive speed, the 5.00 pm Millbay–Penzance service, shown here, left the rails on a right-hand curve. The 0-4-4T No. 3521 can be seen resting against the embankment, whilst the second locomotive 0-4-4T No. 3548 stands at right angles to the line clearly blocking both tracks. Following this accident these Dean '3521' class locomotives were banned from main line duties and double-heading in their case was prohibited.   *Cornwall Local Studies Library*

were also in some seven feet of water. The first class vehicle was thrown furthest from the viaduct and rested on its side on the second class carriage, crushing the rear end, where the leading guard, William Hoskins, was located.

Rear guard Paddon, with the help of two other men then began the rescue of those in the creek below. Scrambling and wading through the mud, the men found that most of these passengers were not seriously injured. They were then taken to nearby houses to be made comfortable and treated. The leading guard was, however, killled in the crash, whilst the driver and fireman also died instantly, their bodies being dug out on the following day. News of the disaster inevitably attracted large numbers of sight-seers over the weekend. It was estimated that over 2,000 people gathered in the area on the Sunday to see what they could of the wreckage.

At the inquest, held at St Germans Police Station on Monday 9th May the surviving guard said that he could not account for the accident in any way, and added that, in his view, the train was not running at any excessive speed. Other witnesses also supported the guard as to the speed, but some referred to a 'jerking or jostling' at or about that location whilst travelling eastward that morning.

A civil engineer with the Company gave evidence that on inspection, he had found a section of track 148 yards east of the viaduct where the track had begun to vent outwards from the effect of the train leaving the line. He could not say what had actually caused the locomotive to do this. The verdict from the inquest was that of accidental death –

The Jury are unable to decide as to the cause of death – but they beg to say that although there is no evidence of neglect on the part of the Company, they should suggest more stringent directions should be given to enginemen to the speed they should observe – more especially while the line is new.'

One week later *The Royal Cornwall Gazette* carried the following related information:

In consequence of the recent accident, the Cornwall Railway Directors have issued a new timetable which gives 10 to 20 minutes longer for travelling between Plymouth and Truro.

The second of the more serious incidents considered here involved the head-on collision of two freight trains between St Germans and Menheniot on 2nd December 1873.

In the early morning, at just after 5.00 am, two goods trains, the 3.15 am 'up' service and the 2.00 am 'down', stood at the Menheniot station. The 'up' train was running late and it was intended to hold it at Menheniot in order to allow the 3.30 pm 'down' goods to run in from St Germans and cross in the station. The 'down' goods actually waiting at Menheniot to proceed to Liskeard was given 'line clear' and instructed to leave. The guard heard the call, 'Alright, Dick,' but the guard of the 'up' goods, also called 'Dick', mistook the clearance assuming it was for him, whereupon he waved away his 'up' train.

The stationmaster immediately telegraphed St Germans warning them to hold their down goods, but by that time it was too late. Both trains were accelerating towards one another, oblivious of the danger. At approximately 5.30 am the two freight trains collided, the incident happening in a cutting near Barrasfill Farm. It was said that the crash was such that it was heard in St Germans itself.

Both trains were heavily laden. The 'up' goods, double-headed by the locomotives *Lance* and *Brutus*, consisted mainly of loaded china clay and china stone wagons numbering about 30 together with other wagons of general merchandise and wool. The 'down' train, headed by the locomotive *Romulus* consisted of general merchandise and a consignment of a number of bullocks being brought west from Highbridge.

The footplate crews were in the greatest danger and following the collision, were trapped under their locomotives with wrecked wagons also piled upon and around them together with their contents. The guards, not badly hurt, went for help. With the assistance of local people they managed, in the darkness and confusion to free those trapped under the locomotives. Injuries were said to be not serious, consisting mainly of shock, bruising and burns. One fireman was described as 'shaken, but not otherwise injured beyond a cut on the head.' Five of the six crew men were then taken to the South Devon Hospital. Many of the bullocks, however, were severely injured, if not dead. Those suffering internal and external injuries were destroyed almost immediately to prevent further suffering. The local press said of the accident:

We are quite within the mark when we say that such a spectacle of complete destruction has never before been presented by the scene of any railway accident in the West.

The newspaper referred to the chaos confined within the cutting. Wagons were crushed, overturned and, in one case, actually hanging half over one of the locomotives. Of the latter, *Lance*, the pilot on the 'up' train, was so badly damaged that it was subsequently withdrawn for scrap, its frames being shattered, the front wheels broken away, and the footplate crushed. The varied contents of the trains were also thrown indiscriminately across the scene. China clay, barrels of beer and consignments of wool, hops, oranges, herrings and nuts added to the general confusion, not forgetting, of course, the sights of sufferings of the helpless livestock.

A special train was sent from Plymouth with the officials of the railway and a travelling crane was brought from St Germans. The work of clearing the line began as soon as was possible and continued day and night. Wreckage and salvaged goods were placed in the fields nearby and passengers and their luggage on normal services were transferred to 'up' and 'down' trains on each side of the accident. Steps were cut in the sides of the cutting to help with the transfer. The line was cleared in time for the down mail on the Wednesday morning.

Starting signals were soon introduced at stations in order to help prevent any further repeat of this kind of accident.

On Monday 18th April 1895 *The Royal Cornwall Gazette* reported a major incident on the main line:

An alarming accident took place on the Cornish section of the Great Western system on Saturday evening at a point about equidistant between Doublebois and Bodmin Road stations. Fortunately no lives were lost, and none of the injuries sustained by either the train staff or the passengers were serious; but all the elements that might have contributed to an appalling catastrophe were present –

The train involved here was the 5.00 pm Millbay to Penzance service and consisted of two locomotives, seven coaches, a meat van and two horse-boxes. At Doublebois the train was running to time, but on leaving for Bodmin Road it descended the bank at what was considered a very fast pace. Midway between the two stations 'a rough jolting was experienced, followed by a violent rocking, and finally, came a sickening thundering crash.'

As the train followed a right curve in the Fowey Valley the leading locomotive, 0-4-4T No. 3521, left the rails, hitting the bank to the left. The second locomotive, No. 3548, also of the same class (Dean '3521') was thrown across the 'up' line at a right angle. Of the rolling stock, only the horse-boxes remained on the rails. The leading coaches sustained most damage, but the press was anxious to pay tribute to the robust nature of the coaching stock:

'The ends of all the carriages bear evidence of the force of the impact, but they also afford splendid evidence of the durability and substantial character of the Great Western rolling stock. Had they not been so well built the whole train must inevitably have telescoped with the results to the passengers almost too dreadful to contemplate.'

With regard to the passengers and staff, it was said that 'beyond severe shakings bruises and cuts of a comparative few and the slight scalding of the drivers and their firemen, all had providentially escaped.'

The track was badly damaged by the crash. To the east, the line beyond the train was twisted and buckled up to a distance of seventy yards, whilst alongside the locomotives sections of track had been severed. Relief gangs were sent to the scene from St Blazey, Lostwithiel and Plymouth. Dr Buchan and the local railway ambulance staff also attended the scene, but local doctors and medical help had already arrived from Bodmin.

Work continued through Saturday night and the following Sunday to clear the line. It was hoped that the 'up' line could be re-laid and open for the mail train on the Sunday evening. To this effect, breakdown gangs from Newton Abbot and Plymouth equipped with a special train gave further assistance on the Sunday. The four de-railed coaches were back on the up line by the Sunday evening and were taken to the sidings at Doublebois. It was not possible to open the line on the Sunday, but it was considered important to enable the Easter Monday holiday traffic to run through.

Initial reactions to the crash revealed bewilderment. The line had been doubled between Doublebois and Bodmin Road in December 1893 and was considered to be in as good a condition as any part of the Great Western system and, furthermore, 'the best section of line west of Exeter.'

Investigations into this crash revealed that the line was likely to have been damaged by the preceding train, the *Cornishman*. The latter was running late at Liskeard, but almost on time, having made up three minutes by Bodmin Road. Estimates gave speeds of up to almost 60 mph, whereas the booked speed was 34 mph. Double-headed 0-4-4T, numbers 3536 and 3537, were the locomotives involved and with the rear engine responsible for the braking, damage was done to the track. Following this accident it was decided that the 0-4-4Ts involved were not to be double-headed and were to be taken off main line duties. Between 1899 and 1902 this class of locomotives was rebuilt as 4-4-0s.

Leaving actual train services, a most serious accident in terms of loss of life took place at Coldrennick Viaduct, immediately east of Menheniot, on 9th February, 1897. Twelve men died there when a platform collapsed during reconstruction work. Eleven died instantly from the fall, whilst the twelfth died within an hour.

The men were at work on wooden staging erected beneath one of the centre spans when, without warning, their platform collapsed. Six other men at work managed to cling to the woodwork on the old viaduct and, thereby, save themselves. All those involved were in the process of placing a new corrugated steel beam into position. It was later stated that only a matter of minutes before, the men had placed a much heavier beam into position without the timber showing any defect. The disaster was the direct result of the collapse of a broken bearer, a length of yellow pine 22 feet long and 8 inches in section. This length of timber was previously a ballast rail belonging to the old viaduct, and on inspection was found to be waterlogged and badly flawed. It had supported the platform on which the men were working.

The inquest, held at the Sportsmans Arms almost immediately alongside Menheniot station, revealed that correct procedures were not followed regarding installation. Thomas Hughes Gibbons, Chief Engineer of the GWR Plymouth Division explained that the bearers, as supporting beams, should have been chained to the main beams of the viaduct thereby reducing the strain put upon them. On investigation it was found that the beam had not been chained, but had it been so, and given that the wood was sound, it should have supported a weight of up to three tons. The Chief Engineer also stated that, in his opinion, the accident would not have happened if his instructions had been followed; the foreman had been told to use chains. The inquest recommended that the GWR should provide printed regulations regarding the use of chains and suitable timbers in connection with work on the viaduct. Foremen and gangers were then to familiarise themselves with such directions.

Following the accident the dead men were taken to the goods shed at Menheniot station. They were all from the immediate area, their ages ranging from 21 to 41 years. Seven of the victims were married, with children.

In November 1897 two men were also killed in the rebuilding of Treviddo Viaduct, between Liskeard and Menheniot. They were installing the woodwork which was to support the new brickwork in the arches. Whilst removing the block and chain used for lifting the supports into position, the ropes broke throwing the two men and the woodwork to the ground, some 75 to 80 feet below. One died instantly, but the other survived long enough to reach Liskeard cottage hospital whereupon he too was found to be dead. An inquest returned a verdict of accidental death.

Chapter Ten

Bodmin Road – Wadebridge: GWR

"Wherever work was to be done, railways were to be constructed, or civilisation had to be pushed forward, there would be the English working man." This classic of later Victorian England, addressed to a gathering of the navvies on the GWR Bodmin branch, was but one of the tributes offered them at the opening ceremonies for the line. Following a substantial celebratory meal of good roast beef, and plum pudding, the Mayor and Corporation gave them a rousing vote of thanks for their excellent work and their general order throughout. GWR investment was also formally recognised in numerous toasts through the Company's representatives, principally, Mr A. Hubbard, Director, Mr H. Lambert, Chief Goods Officer, Paddington, and Mr C. Inglis, Resident Engineer. The town and district, likewise, responded to the great event with the inevitable bands, processions, triumphal arches and fireworks, the line opening on Thursday 26th May 1887.

A branch had been proposed for Bodmin under the Cornwall Railway Act of 1846, but such plans were abandoned in the dire financial climate of 1847, when even the work on the main line suffered. Further attempts were made with regard to the branch, notably, in 1867 and 1873, before eventual success with the Act of 10th August 1882.

In July 1864 for example, the Bodmin Railway Company gained an Act to build the link between the town and the main line. The necessity of a good rail connection was underlined at the time by the press. *The Royal Cornwall Gazette* carried the following statement to coincide with the Company's first ordinary meeting in December 1864.

It is needless to enlarge upon the importance of this small branch line; Bodmin being the county town where the two assizes; the four quarter sessions for the county,

Bodmin Road station seen here looking westward in 1922. Set in an extremely attractive rural location the station is shown in grand condition, well ordered and purposeful. A great deal of work was required to build this junction, the site on the 'down' side needing to be cut into the side of the hill, whilst on the 'up' side considerable in-filling was necessary to make sufficient level ground. The branch to Bodmin opened on 26th May 1887.

Cornwall Local Studies Library

'4575' class 2-6-2T No. 5557 is seen here arriving at Bodmin Road with the 8.10 am departure from Padstow on 19th July 1958. The Southern coaching stock is easily recognised. The 9.05 pm train for Padstow, connecting with the 3.30 pm Paddington–Penzance service, was worked by a Southern locomotive, usually an LSWR 'O2' with appropriate coaching stock. The majority of GWR services worked to Bodmin General and Wadebridge.

P. Gray

No. 4569 climbs away from Bodmin Road on a winding gradient that could be as severe as 1 in 37. The train is the 10.10 am Bodmin Road–Padstow on 4th July 1959. Note the fir trees at the lineside beyond the train, these being a particular feature of this branch line.

P. Gray

Further evidence of the hard climb to Bodmin General. '4500' class No. 4559 works the 4.25 to Bodmin General on 18th April 1960. The line included a succession of cuttings and embankments to lift it up the valley. *P. Gray*

'4500' class No. 4552 is seen here dropping down the steep gradient towards Bodmin Road with loaded wagons of china clay from Wenford Bridge on 27th April 1961. *P. Gray*

Having passed the summit and largely circled part of the town to the west, '4500' class No. 4565 drops down into Bodmin General with the 2.30 pm Bodmin Road–Wadebridge in April 1961.
P. Gray

the election of members for the eastern division of the county, the training of the Cornwall Militia, the meetings of the board of guardians of the Bodmin Union, the monthly County Courts and other public meetings are held; and where the County Courts and other public meetings are held; and where the County Gaol and County Lunatic Asylum and the District Registry of Her Majesty's Court of Probate are located. Large numbers of people are constantly ariving at and departing from Bodmin and the greatest inconvenience is at present felt by the magistrates and public generally from the want of a railway.

Despite such a forceful case for the county town, Bodmin gained nothing from this particular scheme. Money was not forthcoming and the proposals were abandoned. A further attempt at the link followed in 1873 involving two lines; one into the town itself, and a second to form a junction with the Bodmin and Wadebridge Railway. This too came to nothing.

Having gained the Act of 1882, it was hoped that the line might be extended, first to Wadebridge, then beyond to serve the North Cornish coast. The traffic potential for granite, slate and agricultural produce from the district around Camelford, for instance, was not overlooked by the GWR, nor was the likely presence of the LSWR. On the 18th August 1882, of course, the North Cornwall Railway

also obtained its necessary powers to extend westward from Launceston to Wadebridge.

Although the Great Western's Bodmin branch was quite short, at only 3 miles 43 chains, construction was difficult. From the junction to the terminus the line climbed almost 300 feet requiring a gradient as fierce as 1 in 37. Cuttings, embankments and bridges abounded as the line wound its way up to the town, the Engineer being Mr C. Inglis of the GWR, who replaced Mr J. Griffiths when the latter gave up the works after a year or so in charge.

Considerable work was necessary at the junction. A vast tonnage of soil and rock needed to be cut from the hillside on the south, or 'down' side of the main line to provide accommodation for the goods shed and sidings. It was also necessary to raise the level of the land on the north side for the branch itself and for further sidings alongside the main line, the spoil from the cutting being used to make the substantial embankments on the 'up' side.

In addition it was necessary to divert the River Fowey, immediately alongside the station, directing its flow away from the new works on a curve slightly northward of its original course. Lord Robartes' private road between the station and nearby Lanyhdrock House was also affected. The branch line now blocked this access, making it necessary to construct a new road which passed behind the station on the down side, crossing beneath the main line to the west.

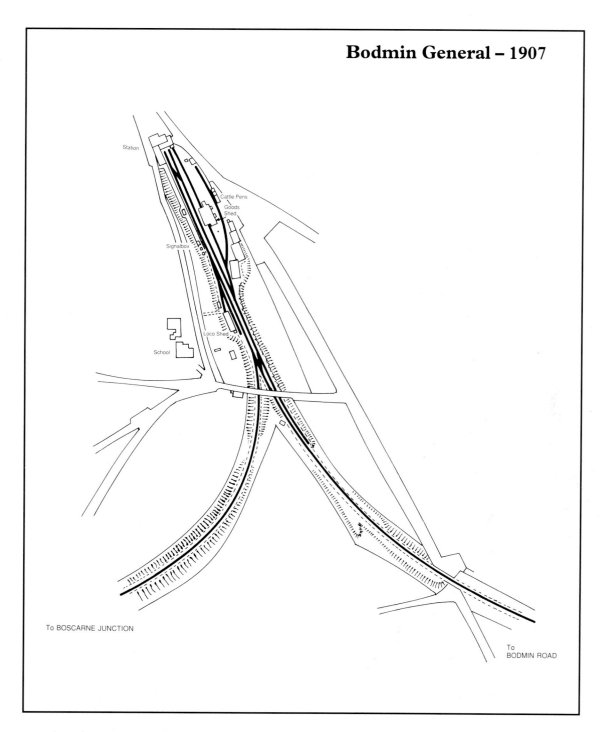

Station

Cattle Pens
Goods
Shed

Signalbox

Loco Shed

School

To BOSCARNE JUNCTION

To
BODMIN ROAD

Messrs Lang and Sons of Liskeard, well known for their work with the Cornwall Railway, took charge of these road works, which included a deep cutting, a retaining wall, a bridge over the River Fowey and a long embankment through the meadowland leading to Lanhydrock. A great deal of planting was also carried out on the slopes of the embankment with trees and shrubs decorating the route, Lord Robartes and the GWR jointly financed the works.

The main buildings at the junction remained on the 'down' side, but new extended facilities were opened on the 'up' and branch platforms for 1887. A new covered footbridge linked both platforms this replacing the wooden crossing provided at rail level. West of the station, on the down side, was the wooden goods shed and adjacent siding;

cattle pens were also provided between the goods shed and the station, with a short loading bay leading in behind the 'down' platform. Prior to the gauge conversion in 1892 standard gauge branch trains ran in alongside the broad gauge mainline, a connection between the two not being possible. By the beginning of 1888 there were ten trains in each direction; the journey time down to the main line at Bodmin Road being 10 minutes, with a thirteen minute journey in the opposite direction for most services.

Leaving Bodmin Road, the line curved northward on a high embankment built over the original course of the river. At the far end of this embankment is a viaduct crossing the river on its new course, the viaduct being of five arches and some sixty feet in height. The embankment continued on

Above: Entering Bodmin General, No. 5539 passes the small locomotive depot and No. 4565 taking water on shed. The train is the 3.24 pm working from Wadebridge. The vee shaped junction mentioned in the text can be seen here. The train entered the picture from beneath a bridge behind the loco depot, the branch can be seen leading off to the right alongside the buffer stop. The route to Bodmin Road was that seen running beneath the bridge in the background, curving away to the left. 18th April 1961. *P. Gray*

Left: China clay working in Bodmin General yard. '4500' class No. 4552 is shunting the first section of its train into sidings before returning to Boscarne Junction for the second portion. The steep gradient as harsh as 1 in 37 made this process necessary. Beyond the train, the goods shed and part of the 'L' shaped terminal building can be seen. The vee junction is clearly illustrated in this view taken from the road bridge in May 1961. *P. Gray*

Boscarne Junction – 1907

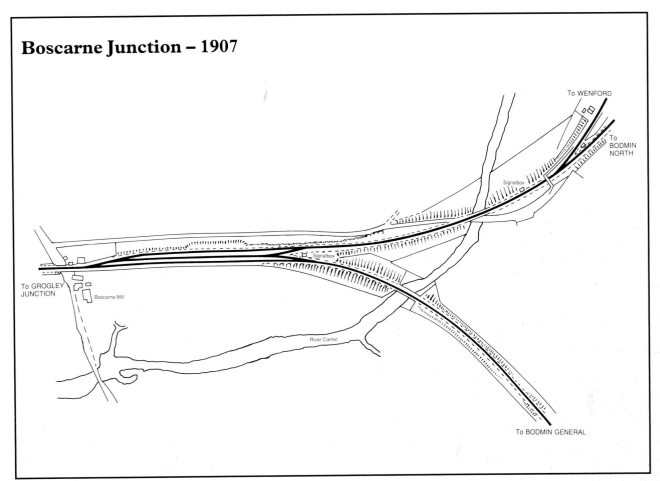

To WENFORD

To BODMIN NORTH

Signalbox

Signalbox

To GROGLEY JUNCTION

Boscarne Mill

River Camel

To BODMIN GENERAL

A fine view of the station, goods shed and locomotive depot is given here as '4500' series No. 4552 leaves Bodmin General with the 12.20 pm Bodmin Road–Wadebridge service, 27th May 1961. Happily Bodmin General is now the home of the Bodmin Steam Railway and the site is once more a stronghold of steam.

P. Gray

'4500' class No. 4565 rounds the curve to enter Bodmin General on 10th September 1960, with the 11.35 am working from Padstow. Note the long embankment curving around on this particular section. Further northward the line also passed through deep cuttings dropping down to Boscarne Junction.

P. Gray

the far side of the viaduct, passing through Dreasonmoor Wood until the rising ground demanded a cutting. Soil from this lengthy cutting was used for the embankment through the woodland. Ascending the valley, the route twice passed beneath the Bodmin-Liskeard Turnpike. On the first occasion, having run alongside the road for a short distance, it passed into a beautifully wooded valley and through open fields east of the road. A further deep cutting then brought the line under the road again to follow a wide curve around the higher ground south of the town. On this final section there was once more a succession of cuttings and embankments carrying the line around to the terminus. West of the line, and just short of the station, came the 'vee' shaped junction where the extension line was to lead down to Boscarne Junction. All trains eventually working the full journey between Bodmin Road and Wadebridge had to reverse at the terminus to gain access to the Wadebridge line.

Situated in a cutting, the GWR station was sited on the west side of the Bodmin-Lostwithiel road close to the army barracks. At a short distance south-west of the town centre the terminus was just below the 400 foot contour and from there the line again descended sharply to Boscarne Junction over its extension, opened on 3rd September, 1888.

Bodmin's GWR terminus was an interesting site. The platform was on the west side of the line with an attractive stone signalbox at its far end. Beyond this again, on the same side, was the stone-built, single road locomotive shed. Nearer to the main terminal building, but on the opposite side of the line, was the goods shed, also in stone and served by a single line. Behind this, again, were the cattle pens. The main station building was designed as an L shape, and was constructed of dressed granite by Thomas Jenkin of Plymouth. Heavy excavation work was required in its construction but here, as on all parts of the line, the GWR was given full cooperation regarding access and land by both the town council and Lord Robartes.

The extension of 2 miles 56 chains from the terminus down to Boscarne Junction was yet another heavily graded section as steep as 1 in 37. From the junction at the entrance to the terminus the line falls continuously to meet the LSWR metals at Boscarne. Like the section from Bodmin Road to the terminus, this also passed through extremely attractive countryside, a particular feature of the route being the GWR's policy of planting fir trees at the lineside.

Under an agreement of 5th June 1886, the Great Western and London South Western companies agreed terms for through services from Bodmin Road to Wadebridge. These also began on 3rd September 1888, but to make this possible the LSWR agreed to reconstruct its route of 4 miles 64 chains from Boscarne to Wadebridge.

Another delightfully rural railway scene as No. 4569 climbs the gradient from Boscarne Junction to Bodmin General. The date is 10th September 1960 and the train, the 1.23 service from Wadebridge–Bodmin Road.

P. Gray

Southern, or LSWR, architecture is apparent here in the shape of the house, signalbox, signals and oil lamps at Nanstallon. The halt was opened on 2nd July 1906. Here, on 10th September 1960, No. 4569 works a train to Wadebridge. Nanstallon was served by certain Western Region trains, but Grogley, also opened on 2nd July, 1906, was served almost entirely by the Bodmin North–Wadebridge/Padstow workings.

P. Gray

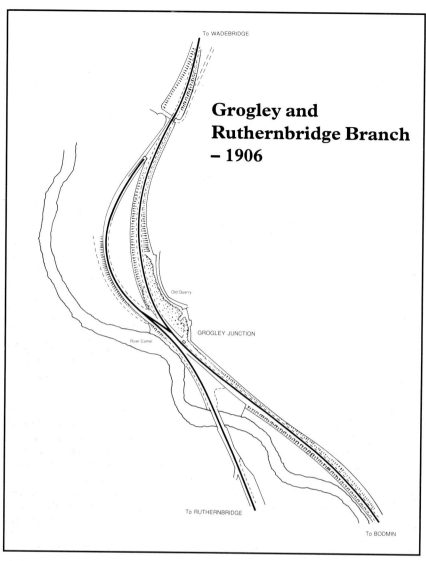

To WADEBRIDGE

**Grogley and
Ruthernbridge Branch
– 1906**

Old Quarry

GROGLEY JUNCTION

River Camel

To RUTHERNBRIDGE

To BODMIN

Passenger services were suspended from 1st November 1886 but there were occasional freight trains. The line was relaid with wooden sleepers and bullhead rail, replacing stone sleepers and inferior track. Messrs Lucas and Aird were the contractors. At Boscarne Junction a signalbox and a house for the signalman was provided. Just under a mile westward, at the junction for the Ruthern Bridge line, (then referred to as Grogley Junction) there was a deviation to avoid a sharp curve. The new curve was slightly to the east of the original line and separated from it by a bank. Access to the Ruthern Bridge line remained on the old alignment, trains having to reverse on to the latter from the Wadebridge direction.

The Ruthern Bridge branch of some 1¼ miles served an iron and ochre mining area, but the line itself also figured largely in plans on the part of standard gauge interests to strike westwards towards Truro.

In July 1865 the Cornwall Central Railway Act gave the necessary powers for a standard gauge line to Truro. It was another attempt to open a central route through the county in conjunction with the London and South Western Railway, and received a good deal of support locally. News of the Act was certainly popular at St Columb, for example. The church bells were rung at length and the local Rifle Corps turned out in full uniform and two barrels of ale were distributed. A grand fete was also planned in celebration of the event. The struggles between the Cornwall Company and the Central Railway of the 1840s have been considered in an earlier chapter, but despite its popularity this particular plan was, ultimately, no more successful than those before or after it.

Eleven years later, the standard gauge Cornwall Minerals Company also pursued a link between their line at Victoria (Roche) and the L&SWR at Ruthern Bridge. The Cornwall Minerals and Bodmin and Wadebridge Junction Railway Bill made good progress through Parliament in 1875/76, but from the following year the CMR, impoverished by a marked depression in the iron ore and clay trades, was worked by the GWR, this being agreed for October 1877. Thus Ruthern Bridge remained a short branch line, eventually seeing its last train in November 1933.

As part of the development of 1888 the LSWR also constructed a new terminus at Wadebridge, the overall costs of the improvements to their line being given as £15,118. The station was described on opening as 'a substantial and commodious building of stone', with a glazed canopy supported by iron pillars. A substantial goods shed and a signalbox were also provided. Details of train working showed that in total there were twelve trains to Wadebridge and eleven to Bodmin including one goods and one mixed working daily. There was no service on Sundays. The GWR worked the line under the 1886 arrangements; they also

GWR and LSWR together! '4500' class 2-6-2T No. 4559 at Wadebridge, with a train for Bodmin Road is alongside LSWR 4-4-0 'T9' No. 30709 destined for the North Cornwall line, Okehampton and Exeter. The photograph from the early 1950s shows Wadebridge for the busy railway centre that it once was. Today the site is covered by a housing development.
P. Treloar

provided booking and goods clerks, and an inspector at Wadebridge. The LSWR provided the rest of the station staff which the GWR paid for in fees. *The Royal Cornwall Gazette* reported that the opening of the line was a somewhat subdued affair and it mentioned a possible division amongst the people – 'Great Western' versus 'South Western' – as the reason for it. Reporting on the opening, the newspaper observed: 'There was no public demonstration at either end of the line, and the first train entered Wadebridge without so much as a cheer to announce its advent.' Leading officials of both companies were present, however. The arrival, proper, of the South Western seven years later over the North Cornwall line intensified the sense of rivalry, as through services to Waterloo were then available.

Whatever rivalry may or may not have existed in 1888, there was no doubt that the new line was a boon to the district. *The Royal Cornwall Gazette* said of the railway that it would 'greatly add to the importance of Wadebridge as a centre for both trade and tourism.' New housing schemes were in hand in anticipation of increased business whilst a regular omnibus service was kept busy linking Padstow in particular.

The official opening of the North Cornwall line to Wadebridge on 12th June 1895, coinciding with the Royal Cornwall Show, brought further obvious development. With the extra services the station was enlarged – an island platform, for instance, being built for the new services. The 1908 plan of the station layout reflected an important railway centre, the quays also handling valuable trade for the railway. From March 1899, of course, Wadebridge was no longer a terminus. In that year the 5½ mile extension along the banks of the River Camel opened to Padstow, giving this attractive resort its long awaited rail links with other parts of Britain. Undoubtedly, the LSWR was now the major influence in the area, the Great Western presence being much less significant. A direct passenger service to Waterloo, valuable tourist traffic for Padstow and the north

coast, via Camelford (for Tintagel and Boscastle) and Port Isaac Road; fishing interests, also from Padstow and Port Isaac; slate from Delable, and, the livestock trade from the area generally, all became identified with South Western interests as the natural outlet for business.

Rivalry between the two railway companies was underlined on the route between Bodmin and Wadebridge, by the turn of the century. Bodmin's South Western terminus was rebuilt, whilst there new halts along the route, at Dunmere, Nanstallon and Grogley, all opened on 2nd July 1906, were not served by Great Western trains. This situation continued into nationalisation; indeed, old company rivalries were upheld throughout the West Country wherever the later Western and Southern Region systems met. During World War Two, however, GWR main line trains did, on occasion, use the branch between Bodmin Road and Wadebridge in order to make use of the Southern Railway between Wadebridge and Exeter. It was a useful emergency route avoiding Plymouth but involved several reversals in the process.

Nationalisation itself did not bring great changes. During September 1949 the ex Southern Region station was designated Bodmin North and the ex GWR station, Bodmin General. In April 1950, the Southern lines west of Exeter were transferred to Western Region control, only to be handed back to the Southern again in 1958. January 1963 saw the Western Region regain final control but by that time the former LSWR system had little future. Churchward '4500' and '4575' class 2-6-2Ts handled Western Region trains between Bodmin Road and Wadebridge until, first North-British class 22 diesel hydraulics and later DMU services took charge. St Blazey depot, 83E, supplied locomotives for the branch workings.

Duplicate services from Bodmin General and Bodmin North were rationalised in 1964 with the opening of Boscarne Exchange Platform. Passengers using the ex Southern terminus travelled to and from Boscarne in a

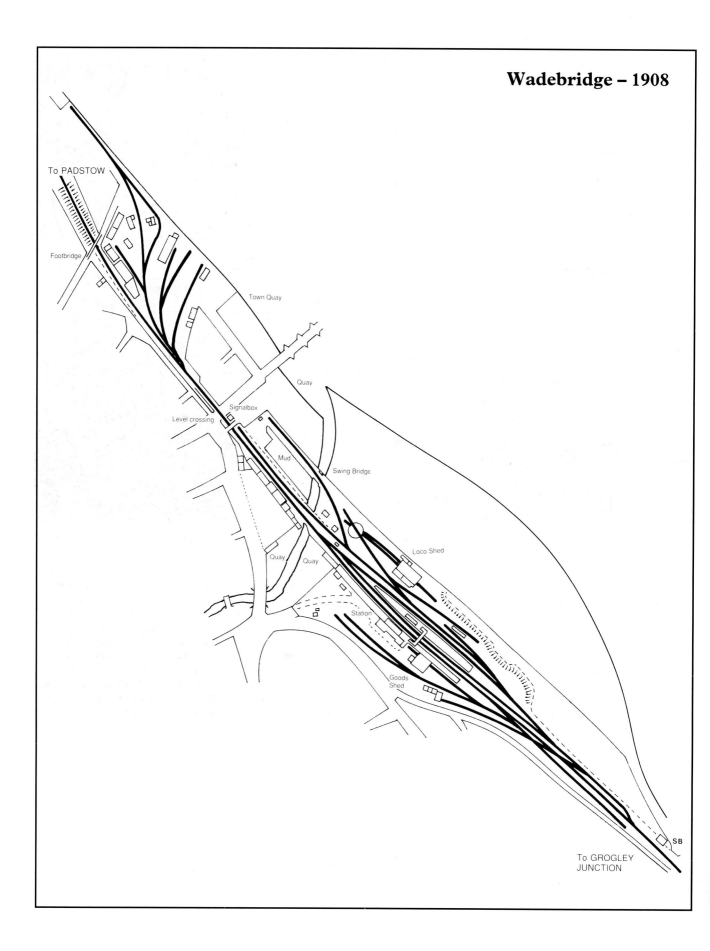

Wadebridge – 1908

To PADSTOW

Footbridge

Town Quay

Quay

Signalbox

Level crossing

Mud

Swing Bridge

Quay   Quay

Loco Shed

Station

Goods
Shed

SB

To GROGLEY
JUNCTION

Not a GWR train, but a GWR locomotive! '5700' class 0-6-0 PT No. 4666 passes the old Bodmin Gaol with the 11.55 am Padstow–Bodmin North service on 13th July 1961.
P. Gray

railbus, there joining the train from Bodmin General. It made for a useful economy but total closure to passengers along the branch was not far off. On 30th January 1967 passenger services between Bodmin Road, Wadebridge and Padstow ceased; the LSWR North Cornwall route had already closed on 3rd October the previous year. Freight traffic between Wadebridge and Bodmin Road continued until January 1979 with the line also seeing several special passenger workings. The Wenford Bridge line narrowly missed 150th anniversary when it too closed in September 1983. Clay traffic had previously kept this charming and early line open.

West of Boscarne the line is now lifted, the trackbed having been converted to an attractive footpath. At Wadebridge the station area and the site of the locomotive depot is now a housing estate, but the actual station building is being adapted as the John Betjeman Centre. Bodmin General is now happily the home of the Bodmin Steam Railway, the Cornish preservation group formed to bring steam back to the heart of Cornwall. Steam trains should once again connect the town with the main line, as at Bodmin Parkway (no longer Bodmin Road) work is proceeding to allow branch trains access to their original platform.